Chrysemys scripta elegans (*Red-eared Slider*)

A PETKEEPER'S GUIDE TO

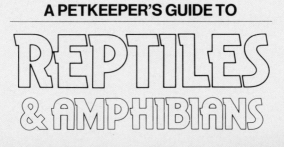

REPTILES
& AMPHIBIANS

Phelsuma cepediana (*Day Gecko*)

No. 16055

Lampropeltis triangulum (*Milk Snake*)

A PETKEEPER'S GUIDE TO

REPTILES

& AMPHIBIANS

A practical introduction to keeping and breeding a wide range of these fascinating creatures

David Alderton

a Salamander book

Published by Salamander Books Limited
LONDON • NEW YORK

A Salamander Book

Hyla arborea (*European Tree Frog*)

Credits

Editor: Geoff Rogers Designer: Roger Hyde
Colour reproductions
Rodney Howe Ltd.
Filmset: SX Composing Ltd.
Printed in Belgium by Henri Proost & Cie, Turnhout.

Author

David Alderton's
abiding interest in the field of pet care
and natural history began with the study of
veterinary medicine at Cambridge University. Now the
author of over 20 books, many with a particular emphasis
on 'exotic pets', David still finds time to contribute
regularly to general and specialist periodicals in the UK
and overseas. In addition to writing, David has always
kept and bred a variety of animals and birds, and now
runs a highly respected service that offers advice on the
needs of animals kept in domestic and
commercial environments.

Contents

Introduction

Not everyone would want to keep a snake as a pet, yet within the reptiles and amphibians (collectively known as herptiles) there is such a diversity of size, colour and appearance that the appeal of keeping these creatures in the domestic environment continues to grow apace. The familiar 'Greek' tortoise has been a popular pet for centuries, with Gilbert White's account of his tortoise Timothy during the eighteenth century being one of the earliest studies of these creatures. Today, keeping 'exotic' pets has never been easier, particularly with the help of sophisticated electrical gadgets to create the right environmental conditions. Now it is possible not only to maintain herptiles in captivity, but also to breed them.

An 'enclosure' or 'container' used for keeping reptiles and amphibians is called a vivarium and a suitably decorated vivarium can form an attractive focal point in a room in the same way as a well-furnished aquarium. The connection with the fishkeeping

hobby goes even further, for much of the equipment and foodstuffs produced for fishes are equally suitable for reptiles and amphibians. You can obtain these essential supplies from many pet stores, even if they do not stock herptiles.

In many ways, herptiles are ideal pets: their needs are not particularly time-consuming; they can be accommodated where space is too limited to keep other pets; the vast majority are neither noisy nor smelly and they do not need feeding every day – a distinct advantage at holiday times. Nevertheless, you should not leave herptiles on their own for long periods in case an accident happens, such as a terrapin becoming overturned and being unable to right itself, or an electrical breakdown occurs.

Keeping herptiles can become an absorbing passion. Indeed, the observations of many amateur 'herpetologists' have greatly added to our knowledge of these fascinating creatures.

Basic biology

The amphibians are considered by zoologists to be the more primitive of the two classes, showing certain affinities with fishes. Fossil records show that this group has existed for more than four hundred million years. The aquatic origins of amphibians are still clearly apparent in many species today, with some spending much of their lives in water. The skin of amphibians needs to be kept moist because, although they have lungs, they also 'breathe' through the skin. Since they need a large surface area relative to their overall volume, this immediately places a restraint on their size. Reptiles rely solely on their lungs for respiration, so they can grow significantly larger.

Both classes of herptile are poikilothermic (commonly, but misleadingly, known as cold-blooded), which means that they are unable to regulate their body temperature independently of the environment. As a result, the majority of species are confined to tropical areas and the reptiles especially are typically 'sun-seeking'. Amphibians, with their sensitive skins, tend to be more secretive and remain in suitably moist localities away from sunlight.

Above: *The skin of amphibians is covered with mucus glands that help to keep the surface moist and shiny.*

Below: *The skin of reptiles is quite dry and scaly, and serves to restrict water loss from the body.*

Hibernation

In the wild, as the temperature falls in temperate regions, so the availability of food for herptiles also declines. Faced with these problems, herptiles enter a period of dormancy known as hibernation. Body temperature falls and the metabolic rate slows, so that hibernating animals have a very low requirement for food and are able to depend upon fat stores built up over the previous summer to sustain themselves.

Herptiles from tropical climates may also undergo similar periods of dormancy when environmental conditions are unfavourable. Hingeback Tortoises, for example, burrow during periods of dry weather, emerging only at the onset of the next rainy period.

There are a number of popular misconceptions about hibernation. It is not, for example, harmful if a species that normally hibernates is kept awake over the winter, providing adequate food and water is available. Indeed, it would be

Below: Reptiles in the wild often seek out warm spots, such as rocks heated by the sun's rays, in order to maintain their body temperature.

**Typical reptile
life cycle**

Courtship in tortoises is
usually aggressive, with the
male biting at exposed parts
of the female's body

5   It can take eight years
or more for land
tortoises to mature

After a variable hatching
period, youngsters take
several days to break out

Mating takes place   2
shortly afterwards

4

Eggs are then buried in a nest dug
by the female. She may lay fertile eggs
for several years after mating

3

foolhardy to hibernate a young
tortoise hatched in autumn over the
following winter. If an animal
awakes prematurely it will not die as
a result.

On emerging from hibernation,
the herptiles will have lost weight,
and part of this weight can be
accounted for by water. Reptiles will
normally drink more when they
come out of hibernation, and it is
particularly beneficial if you give
them a soluble vitamin preparation
at this time. Offering fruit or thawed
deep-frozen tomatoes are other
means of rehydrating reptiles. In
amphibians especially, studies have
shown that hibernation is extremely
important in the breeding cycle. It
has proved possible to artificially
manipulate this seasonal response
in order to stimulate reproduction,
as discussed on page 45.

Reproduction
The reproductive behaviour of
amphibians and reptiles differs
significantly. Unlike the majority of

Above: *Fertilization in reptiles takes
place within the female's body. Most
lay eggs; some bear live young.*

reptiles, amphibians have remained
closely tied to water for breeding
purposes. Nevertheless, some
species – such as the Poison Arrow
Frogs (page 102) – have reduced
this dependence to a minimum. In
these frogs, the eggs are fertilized
out of the water and the male then
carries the eggs (and ultimately the
tadpoles) on his back. Finally, he
deposits the tadpoles into a suitable
puddle of water in order to complete
their development.

Mating in reptiles involves internal
fertilization and the resulting eggs
are protected against dehydration
by a shell, which is variable in
texture. Some species give birth to
live young; the eggs are held in the
female's body until they are ready to
hatch. In either case, the young
reptiles emerge from the egg as
miniature adults rather than as a
larval stage in a life cycle.

**Typical amphibian
life cycle**

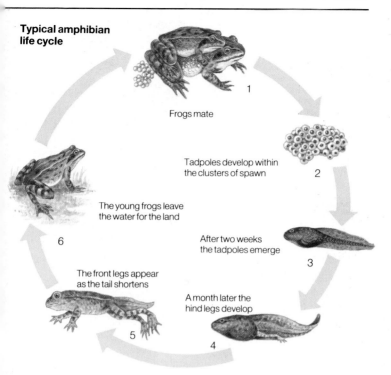

1

Frogs mate

Tadpoles develop within
the clusters of spawn

2

The young frogs leave
the water for the land

6

After two weeks
the tadpoles emerge

3

The front legs appear
as the tail shortens

A month later the
hind legs develop

5

4

Above: *Amphibians usually mate and
lay their eggs in water, where the
tadpoles then develop into adults.*

Below: *The mating grip of frogs and
toads – the amplexus. Vast numbers
of mating individuals may congregate.*

15

Obtaining and handling herptiles

A number of herptiles are caught in the wild and shipped overseas. Such international trade is controlled by the Convention of International Trade in Endangered Species of Fauna and Flora (CITES). In addition, there are likely to be agreements that restrict the taking of native species; the Berne Convention in Europe is one such agreement. The deliberate release of non-native herptiles is also outlawed in many countries, as they may establish themselves and threaten native species. Other regulations control the keeping of poisonous species, notably snakes, which are not included in this book.

The trade in herptiles is often criticised, yet these creatures travel well by air, being packed under prescribed guidelines laid down by the International Air Transport Association. And many herptiles are so abundant in the wild that trade does not seriously affect their numbers. They have a very high reproductive rate in many cases, with correspondingly huge natural losses. Out of the thousands of eggs laid by a frog, for example, only a handful of the resulting offspring will themselves survive to breed.

Where species are threatened, controlled trapping can actually assist their conservation, since the local people protect the herptiles because of their 'commercial' value. The 'Greek' tortoise is a case in point. It used to be exported and was valued accordingly, but now is seen as a pest in some areas; tortoises are being used as living hard core and also as meat in processing plants. The positive conservation benefits of international trade are shown by the actions of certain Turkish farmers. They check that the ponds where European Tree Frogs and Green Toads breed contain sufficient water through the summer to enable the tadpoles to complete their metamorphosis. The farmers catch some of the resulting frogs and sell them abroad, thus ensuring a safe refuge for the population as a whole. Both the habitat and the creatures are conserved by this means.

Above: *A stretch of typical reptile habitat in Queensland, Australia.*

Right: *Transportation methods depend upon the species concerned. Here, Axolotls are safely packed in a plastic bag with plenty of air.*

Obtaining herptiles

There are various means of obtaining herptiles, and to some extent the method is influenced by the species required. Importers usually have a selection of stock throughout the year, but supplies tend to be seasonal, so you may find it difficult to obtain a particular species at a given time. In some instances, you may have a problem persuading imported wild-caught herptiles to transfer to substitute diets, and it is always worth asking what they are being fed on.

You can obtain captive-bred stock from dealers or direct from the breeders concerned. The various herpetological society publications provide valuable information on possible sources. Herptiles bred in captivity – although slightly more expensive in the first instance – are likely to be easier to manage and

should be relatively free from parasitic diseases.

It may be possible to complete the purchase without seeing the herptiles and then have them sent direct, but it can prove very useful to collect them personally. This applies particularly in cold weather, when you can take precautions to prevent them contracting a chill en route. You can transport the majority of herptiles safely in a suitably stout box lined with shredded or crumpled newspaper. Or you can use a cat carrier from which they cannot escape. Damp moss makes the most suitable substrate for amphibians, until they reach their permanent quarters.

Herptiles generally should appear lively, with their eyes open when they are kept at the correct temperature. Some lizards may be missing part of their tail; this is shed as a safety mechanism against predators. It will regrow gradually over a period of time, but until then they are described as stump-tailed. The size of the individual is largely a matter of personal preference; large specimens cost correspondingly more than hatchlings. In some cases, the length is described as SVL, which stands for snout to vent length, and thus excludes the tail.

Above: *Large lizards, such as this iguana, have powerful claws that can present a hazard during handling.*

Above right: *Restrain snakes firmly but never grip them tightly; this can bruise them and may prove fatal.*

Below: *Restrain smaller lizards gently as shown here; some may shed their tails if handled roughly.*

Handling herptiles safely

Never handle herptiles more than absolutely necessary. This is especially important for amphibians, which have sensitive skins. Excessive or rough handling can give rise to the infection known as 'red leg', particularly in frogs and toads. Never handle an amphibian with dry hands, as this is very likely to damage the skin. Some species of amphibians, especially the more brightly coloured ones, produce toxic skin secretions that can be intensely irritating to the eyes, and may also cause problems if the chemical enters by way of a skin wound. It is usually possible to coax individuals carefully into a suitable container when they need to be caught. A fish net is useful for catching aquatic amphibians, although they may also be driven into a plastic bag immersed in the water of their aquatic vivarium.

Chelonians (tortoises, terrapins and turtles) are not difficult to handle, although larger individuals may struggle, and they have surprisingly powerful legs. Be careful to hold these herptiles well away from your clothing; they tend to defaecate without prior warning, especially when they are not used to being handled.

Small lizards, with their quick darting movements, can be a problem to catch, but you can usually persuade them to enter a net without too much trouble. Once caught, the best way to hold a lizard is to gently restrain it by holding your thumb over the neck and wrapping the body in the palm of your hand with your fingers. A similar grip is useful with newts and salamanders, but to hold large lizards, such as iguanas, tegus and monitors, and smaller crocodilians you will need a stout pair of gauntlets. These creatures can inflict painful injuries both with their teeth and claws, and they will also lash out with the tail, so be sure to restrain this too.

Hold snakes with one hand around the neck and use the other hand to restrain the body. Like all reptiles, snakes are likely to resent handling if they are not used to it. Take particular care with larger individuals, especially Boa Constrictors, since these are capable of suffocating you if they wrap themselves around your neck. The body of a snake is sensitive, however, and so never grip it tightly; this can cause internal bruising that will kill the snake within a fortnight. Contrary to popular opinion, snakes are not slimy but have dry skins.

Accommodating herptiles

There is no standard means of housing reptiles and amphibians, since the set-up will be influenced by the habits of the individual species concerned. Tortoises, for example, need a relatively large floor area, and the height of their enclosure is less significant; tree frogs, on the other hand, need a tall vivarium. Before you buy a particular species, therefore, you should find out as much as possible about it, since accommodating it may prove very expensive. Certain reptiles, notably terrapins and some lizards, such as green iguanas and monitors, will grow surprisingly fast when they are fed and housed correctly. As a result, they will rapidly outgrow small enclosures. It is more economical, therefore, to

Below: *Constructing vivariums of such striking design has been made possible by the excellent bonding qualities of silicone rubber sealant.*

provide relatively spacious accommodation from the outset.

In some countries, notably in the USA, Canada and parts of Europe, pet stores and specialist suppliers offer a wide range of purpose-built vivariums for keeping herptiles. Where such supplies are not available, a little ingenuity is called for. Here, we consider some options.

Simple containers
For housing small hardy creatures, try plant propagators available from garden centres. Choose those with a mesh-type ventilator in the lid, to reduce the risk of accidental escapes through a hatch. Alternatively, tape the ventilator panels in place. These very small and simple containers can be difficult to heat, however, even with an aquarium heater. You may resort to using them to raise insects, such as mealworms, for feeding to your herptiles. (See Feeding, page 36.)

To create a warmer environment, use a heated plant propagator. These operate on low voltage and generate a base temperature of about 20°C (68°F), although the air temperature in the unit will also be affected by its position in the room.

If you wish to keep even moderately sized herptiles you will need to investigate further types of containers as possible vivariums. Since your choice will rest on whether you wish to keep aquatic or terrestrial herptiles, let us look at the basic structural requirements for each type in more detail.

Below: *This type of vivarium is most suitable for terrapins or, on a larger scale, for young caimans. It provides both a basking area and adequate space for swimming. Where the water depth allows, position the heater-thermostat in a vertical position. Always use a relatively deep tank; about 45cm (18in) is ideal.*

Catering for aquatic herptiles

The most popular option for housing aquatic herptiles is to convert an aquarium, using a specially designed lid. These are produced in various sizes corresponding to the dimensions of standard tanks. A typical lid of this type has a sliding plastic door, a ventilation grill and a hole for a light fitment.

It is relatively easy to partition an aquarium into 'wet' and 'dry' areas. The area of land relative to water depends on the habits of the particular species concerned. Soft-shelled Turtles, for example, are almost totally aquatic, whereas the Red-eared Terrapins will spend considerable periods out of the water basking under a suitable lamp. Divide the tank by fixing pieces of glass or plastic in position with silicone aquarium sealant and fill the 'wet' area with water to the desired level. Fill the 'dry' area with clean gravel. Since the vivarium

A vivarium for aquatic herptiles

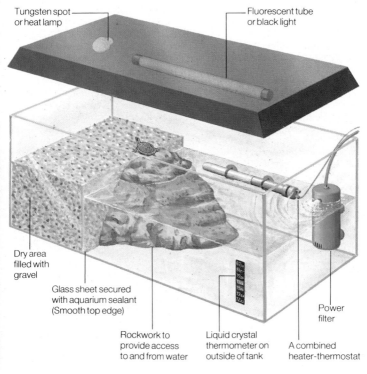

Tungsten spot or heat lamp

Fluorescent tube or black light

Dry area filled with gravel

Glass sheet secured with aquarium sealant (Smooth top edge)

Rockwork to provide access to and from water

Liquid crystal thermometer on outside of tank

Power filter

A combined heater-thermostat

A vivarium for terrestrial herptiles

Daylight fluorescent tube for balanced light

Wooden panel to support and conceal tube

Melamine interior: joints sealed with aquarium sealant

Clear acrylic sliding doors mounted on runners

Sliding floor tray with substrate on top for easy cleaning

Removable central partition

This basic vivarium for terrestrial herptiles can be custom built using easily available materials. Always ensure that the interior is accessible and easy to keep clean.

occupants will need easy access into and out of the water, provide a ramp between the two areas.

Making a terrestrial vivarium

Fish tanks are unsuitable for housing larger and more active terrestrial herptiles. To create an ideal environment for such creatures you will probably need to build a vivarium from scratch. This is not a particularly difficult task, and the resulting unit can prove both attractive and functional.

When you are considering the design always allow for ease of servicing; the finished vivarium must be easy to clean and yet be escape-proof. Geckos prove particularly adept at escaping through a very small gap, for example, as they can run up and down vertical surfaces without difficulty. Snakes also are surprisingly fast, and once loose in a room will frequently disappear beneath the floorboards or into a similarly inaccessible site.

With easy cleaning in mind, consider making your vivarium from sheets of chipboard laminated with a smooth plastic surface. Melamine

covered shelving boards are ideal and are available in white and various colours. Seal all the joints between the panels with silicone aquarium sealant. This will ensure that no debris or parasites can accumulate in the cracks, and means that you can hose out the whole structure without saturating the woodwork. Silicone sealant has a very strong bonding capacity and is now used extensively in the

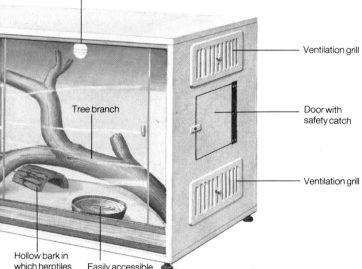

'Natural' spotlight or infrared heater to enable herptile to bask beneath

Ventilation grill

Door with safety catch

Ventilation grill

Tree branch

Hollow bark in which herptiles can hide

Easily accessible water container

manufacture of fish tanks. You can buy it at aquarist or pet stores and similar outlets, and full instructions for use are given on the pack. Do not use sealing products intended for use in bathrooms; they may contain chemicals (such as fungus

Below: *These vivariums consist of simple glass-fronted containers mounted on bookshelves. They provide an aquarium-like display.*

inhibitors) that could prove toxic to herptiles in a vivarium.

Fit a removable tray in the floor of the vivarium so that you can slide this out and clean it without opening the door. As far as doors are concerned, you have several choices. To gain access with the minimum risk of an accidental escape fit hinged flaps in the top or side of the unit. In combination with these, fit sliding doors at the front of the vivarium to give you plenty of room to put in decor and food, and also to clean the unit thoroughly. Use plastic or wooden runners for the sliding doors; aluminium tracks can be scratched by sharp claws, producing dangerous splinters. Ideally, use transparent acrylic rather than glass for the doors; some tortoises in particular will bang repeatedly on transparent surfaces and may injure themselves if the glass breaks. You can buy acrylic sheets in various thicknesses and most suppliers will cut it to size. If the cut edges are rough, smooth them over with glasspaper to prevent possible injury to the vivarium occupants.

Heating and lighting

Providing adequate warmth in the vivarium is vital, particularly for maintaining the appetite of herptiles and increasing their resistance to disease. Lighting also influences the well-being of herptiles and can have a profound effect on their reproductive behaviour. It is not always possible to separate these two factors, particularly if incandescent lamps are being used as both a source of light and heat. To maintain the temperature in the vivarium, it is often necessary to keep such lamps on for much of the time. Such a situation is not ideal, since prolonged exposure to light interferes with the natural rhythm of light and darkness, the so-called photoperiod, that influences the breeding cycle in many species. In addition, evidence suggests that subjecting herptiles to almost constant illumination may well damage their eyesight over a period of time. It is preferable, therefore, to provide heat and light separately within the vivarium.

Heating an aquatic vivarium

The best way of heating the water in an aquatic vivarium is to use a standard heater-thermostat unit familiar to fishkeepers the world over. Follow the maker's installation instructions. Always ensure that the unit is immersed in water whenever it is switched on. For use in a vivarium, wrap the whole unit in a tube of plastic-coated mesh, tied in place where necessary. This may restrict the free circulation of water but it will prevent the herptiles burning themselves if they rest on the heating element. Fix a thermometer to the front of the tank – the digital liquid crystal types are accurate and easy to read – to monitor the temperature in the vivarium. Attach this type of thermometer to the *outside* of the glass. (Here it will be convenient to

Heating systems for aquatic vivarium

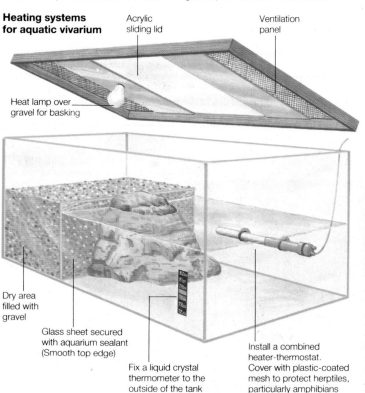

Acrylic sliding lid

Ventilation panel

Heat lamp over gravel for basking

Dry area filled with gravel

Glass sheet secured with aquarium sealant (Smooth top edge)

Fix a liquid crystal thermometer to the outside of the tank

Install a combined heater-thermostat. Cover with plastic-coated mesh to protect herptiles, particularly amphibians

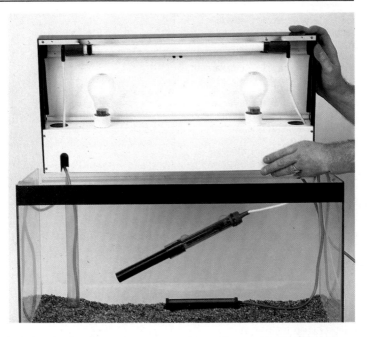

Left: *An aquarium heater-thermostat provides the best means of heating water for herptiles. Include a heat lamp above a suitable basking area.*

Above: *The combination of tungsten and fluorescent lighting in this hood is equally suitable for keeping tropical fishes or aquatic herptiles.*

read but unfortunately open to temporary disturbance by curious fingers.) Most heater-thermostats have an adjustment knob to allow you to change the temperature settings within a limited range.

Heating a terrestrial vivarium

The ideal way of heating a terrestrial vivarium is to use a ceramic infrared heater, which emits warmth but not light. They are available in various wattages; the choice depends on the size and location of your vivarium. Fix the heater into the roof, preferably close to one end so that a temperature gradient builds up within the vivarium. This enables the occupants to move away from the heat source as their body temperature rises. Such behaviour is normal in the wild, being particularly noticeable in Lacertid lizards (e.g. Green Lizard, page 84).

Connect the heater to a reliable thermostat. This will switch the power off once the vivarium reaches

the required temperature. The temperature required varies according to the species, but will generally be within the range of 20-30°C (68-86°F). Although reptiles in particular often come from hot areas, they can be killed if the temperature rises too high. To keep a check on the temperature within the vivarium, fix digital liquid crystal thermometers to the front and at each end of the vivarium, so that they will reveal the temperature gradient inside.

You may need to protect the sides of the vivarium near the heat source with an asbestos substitute. And enclosing the heater in a wire mesh will prevent the occupants burning themselves. This applies especially to lizards, such as geckos, that can walk up the sides of a vivarium with surprising ease, although any arboreal herptile is at risk.

In the wild, reptiles will often seek out a warm spot where the ground has been heated by the sun's rays.

For this reason, always include a paved area in a tortoise paddock. You can create the equivalent effect in the vivarium by installing basking rocks, which have a heating element fitted inside them. Some rocks of this type do become excessively warm, so do ensure that there is no risk of the reptiles being burnt. Another safer, less conspicuous option is to provide a heating pad on the floor of the vivarium. These are produced both for use with animals and plants. Manufactured in either metal or plastic, they consist of a pad with a heating element fitted beneath. Such pads operate off a low wattage and are quite safe, even if they become soiled. You will need to remove and wipe soiled pads occasionally, however.

Another horticultural product that can provide useful bottom heat is a soil warming cable. This acts like a flexible heating element as electrical current passes through the cable. Unfortunately, there is a distinct

Above: *A selection of heat sources for use in a vivarium: a ceramic heater with reflector, a spotlamp, and an under-substrate heating pad.*

Above right: *Suitable vivarium lights: a Grolux tube in a custom-made hood, a warm white tube, and a high UV-output black light tube.*

Below: *A typical set-up for Box Tortoises. Ensure that they can enter and leave the water dish easily. In this vivarium, they can be overwintered without being hibernated.*

Vivarium for Box Tortoises

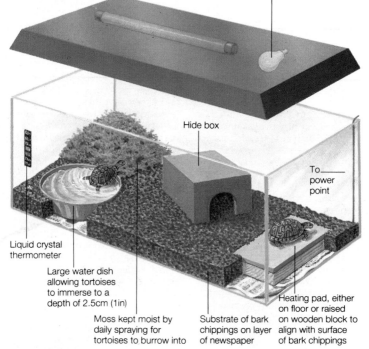

Heat lamp

Hide box

To power point

Liquid crystal thermometer

Large water dish allowing tortoises to immerse to a depth of 2.5cm (1in)

Moss kept moist by daily spraying for tortoises to burrow into

Substrate of bark chippings on layer of newspaper

Heating pad, either on floor or raised on wooden block to align with surface of bark chippings

possibility that buried cables will be disturbed by herptiles burrowing into the substrate. You can fix the cable beneath the base of the vivarium, but the heat transference may not be very satisfactory. Since only part of the floor needs to be warmed in most cases, heating pads are probably the most practical way of providing localised bottom heat. Such heating systems on their own are unlikely to keep the vivarium at the required temperature, however, and should be viewed merely as auxiliary means of providing warmth.

Lighting in the vivarium
Whereas amphibians generally avoid bright sunlight, preferring damp dark spots where there is less risk of dehydration, and some reptiles burrow or are nocturnal, many lizards and chelonians need exposure to daylight if they are to remain in good health. Thus, both the quantity and quality of the light provided in the vivarium are particularly important.

The ultraviolet rays in sunlight stimulate the synthesis of Vitamin D_3 in the skin. This vitamin is vital for mobilising and controlling the stores of calcium and phosphorous in the body. Unfortunately, ultraviolet light is generally filtered out by glass and plastic, so herptiles housed in indoor vivariums are likely to suffer from a deficiency of this essential vitamin. While it is possible to provide Vitamin D_3 in the diet,

correct lighting does appear to act as an appetite stimulant.

Special lights that provide the wavelengths of light present in sunlight are infinitely preferable to ordinary domestic lamps for vivarium use. In addition, conventional tungsten bulbs give out a great deal of heat and can interfere with temperature control. Daylight-type lamps are available in the form of spot-bulbs and fluorescent tubes, and are marketed under various brand names. They are available in various lengths and are easy to incorporate into most vivariums using suitable brackets. Some tubes incorporate a power twist, and these emit more light for a given wattage than a standard tube.

Another form of lighting has been attracting increasing interest from herpetologists over the past few years. Known as black light tubes, they have been used by entomologists investigating nocturnal insects for a considerable period of time. As their name suggests, these fluorescent tubes do not produce light of high intensity, but they have an increased output in the ultraviolet range compared with daylight tubes. To illuminate a vivarium you will need to use black light tubes in conjunction with an ordinary fluorescent tube. As with the daylight tubes, the output of ultraviolet light from black light tubes decreases over a period of time, falling off at the rate of about five percent per year.

Furnishing the vivarium

Having bought or constructed a suitable vivarium and fitted any necessary heating and lighting systems, how do you furnish it to make your herptiles feel completely 'at home'? Here we look at floor coverings, vivarium decor and the possibility of introducing real plants to create a truly living environment.

Floor coverings

Cleanliness is a paramount concern in keeping herptiles. Unsuitable conditions can cause problems – skin infections, for example, which can rapidly become serious. Choose a floor covering, therefore, that is easy to clean and not likely to injure the occupants of the vivarium. Avoid sand of any kind; its fine particles will cling to food, particularly fruit and vegetables, and may be ingested. There are numerous cases of reptiles dying from gut problems caused by ingesting sand.

Coarse gravel is suitable, either in an aquatic or terrestrial set-up. It will need to be thoroughly cleaned,

however, since even prewashed gravel is dirty and will often cloud the water. It may also contain harmful microorganisms. Wash the gravel by rinsing small amounts in a plastic colander under a running tap. Then leave the gravel to stand overnight in a solution of potassium permanganate. This acts as a disinfectant; the water in the bucket should be deep purple in colour. Finally, wash the gravel in running water until the water is clear. Then transfer it to the tank or allow it to dry on sheets of newspaper before using it in a terrestrial setting.

Gravel is essential if an undergravel filtration system is being used for aquatic herptiles. An undergravel filter consists of a perforated plastic plate that fits over the entire floor area of the tank. The

Below: *This set-up for aquatic amphibians incorporates an undergravel filter and an ideal selection of furnishings. The choice of plants will depend on the water temperature and the species kept.*

A furnished vivarium for aquatic amphibians

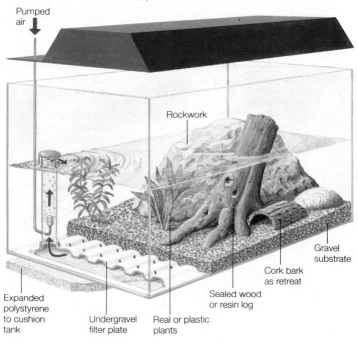

Pumped air

Rockwork

Gravel substrate

Cork bark as retreat

Sealed wood or resin log

Real or plastic plants

Undergravel filter plate

Expanded polystyrene to cushion tank

28

gravel – ideally with a particle size of 3-4mm (0.125-0.16in) – forms a filter bed over the plate to a depth of at least 7.5cm (3in). When the filter plate is connected to an air pump a current is set up that draws water from the tank down through the gravel bed to the space beneath the plate. Channels in the base of the plate conduct the water to one or more 'lift' tubes (the number depends on the size of the plate) that return it to the top of the tank, so setting up a circulation.

The gravel acts not only as a mechanical filter but also as a biological one; a colony of bacteria builds up in the gravel that degrades toxic ammonia waste products to less harmful nitrates.

You will need to remove and wash gravel at regular intervals as it becomes soiled. With relatively messy reptiles, such as tortoises, you may find newspaper or paper towelling a more convenient form of bedding. Although not so attractive, such floor coverings are much easier to change every day. Many

reptiles like to burrow into the base of their vivarium, and granulated paper bedding spread over layers of newspaper is ideal for this purpose. Try to avoid using coarse wood shavings, since these may damage the eyes.

You can use packaged peat and shredded bark in a similar way to granulated paper. These types of bedding are relatively sterile; other organic materials may provide an ideal medium for the development of harmful microorganisms, especially if the ventilation in the vivarium is poor. For this reason, do not use any soil.

Vivarium decor
Many herptiles are relatively shy creatures and need suitable retreats within the vivarium. Decor therefore assumes a practical as well as simply an aesthetic role. Cork bark is popular among herpetologists. You can position pieces on the floor of the vivarium to provide suitable hiding places beneath. Alternatively, use the special wood sold in

Above: *A Crested Newt swims above the gravel substrate in this vivarium. Colonies of aerobic bacteria develop* *within the gravel and purify the water as it passes through the substrate in a continuous circulation.*

aquarist stores. Ideally, seal the cracks and crevices with a coat of polyurethane varnish to exclude parasites. Allow it to dry completely before placing it in the vivarium. Very realistic moulded-resin substitutes are also available.

Rockwork is probably less significant in the context of a vivarium than suitable wood. If you are going to incorporate rockwork always use smooth stones in preference to cement, which can damage the sensitive skins of amphibians in particular. Scrub any rocks destined for the vivarium in a solution of povidine iodine. (This disinfectant/antiseptic is available from pharmacists.) For reptiles you will need to repeat this at regular intervals; the whitish component of their droppings will soon stain rockwork and make it unsightly.

Various other materials may be usefully included in the vivarium. Lengths of plastic tubing, for example, provide ideal retreats for lizards and may serve as sites where eggs will be laid. Whatever materials you use, always arrange the decor within the vivarium so that it cannot injure the occupants. Never balance rocks on top of one another, for example, and fix woodwork in place with dabs of silicone aquarium sealant where necessary.

Plants in the vivarium

Choosing plants suitable for a vivarium depends on the size of the enclosure, the type of environment it provides and, in many cases, on the animals it houses. Herbivorous lizards and tortoises, for example, are likely to destroy plants. And terrapins will damage plants and prevent them rooting in the tank. The answer for terrapins is to use a selection of the superbly realistic plastic plants available for aquariums.

Aquatic amphibians need plants in their vivarium to provide cover and to act as spawning sites. You should be able to choose suitable plants from those sold in aquatic stores. Be sure to wash the plants thoroughly before putting them in the tank, as a precaution against

Above: *Many amphibians spend much time on land, periodically immersing themselves in water to keep their delicate skins moist. Here, a frog takes a dip in a bromeliad.*

Right: *A planted vivarium provides an attractive focus in the home. It will need constant care, however, to keep it looking at its best. Provide ventilation to prevent moulds growing in such a warm, humid environment.*

Below: *To prevent plant roots blocking an undergravel filter plate, contain them in small pots as here.*

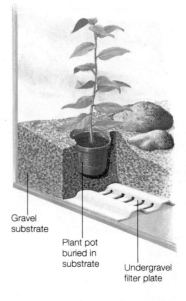

Gravel substrate

Plant pot buried in substrate

Undergravel filter plate

introducing disease organisms and parasites. To choose the most suitable species of plants you will need to consider the temperature of the water and the depth of the tank. Your dealer should be able to advise you on the best species.

Set the plants in small pots, rather than directly into the substrate. The pots will contain rampant root growth and prevent the pores of an undergravel filter from becoming blocked. It also creates less disturbance when you are cleaning out the tank if you can lift out the plants in their individual pots and replace them carefully when you have finished.

For terrestrial vivariums the so-called 'air plants' have become very popular. These members of the bromeliad family grow with little root support and absorb moisture through their leaves. They are very easy to cultivate, requiring no soil or similar growing medium, and you can glue them in position with aquarium sealant. Spray them gently with clean water twice a week to keep them healthy and to maintain a reasonable degree of humidity within the vivarium. You can buy 'air plants', such as *Tillandsia* species, already mounted on bogwood.

If you want to use more traditional house plants, leave these in their pots rather than planting them directly in the substrate. In a vivarium at least 45cm (18in) deep with a substrate covering of about 15cm (6in) you can bury the pots out of sight. Water the plants regularly and remove any dead leaves or shoots before they damp off, which often indicates poor ventilation.

31

General maintenance

Once you have set up all the components of your vivarium, check the system to ensure that the heaters and other electrical appliances are functioning correctly. If in doubt, ask a qualified electrician to sort out the wiring and make everything safe.

Aquatic plants will take at least a week to establish themselves, and so leave the tank unoccupied for this period. There is no need to remove chlorine from tapwater, either by using special chemicals or leaving it to stand for a day or so. Although this is essential when moving fishes to a new environment, some herpetologists are convinced that transferring anurans to fresh tapwater will reduce the risk of the disease known as 'red leg'.

Although both plants and herptiles will benefit from limited exposure to sunlight, never place an enclosed vivarium in direct sunlight. The temperature inside is likely to rise rapidly, with fatal results. Ideally, position the unit near a power point and at a convenient height for servicing the interior.

Day-to-day management
When the occupants of your vivarium are well established, there should be few problems providing you keep their environment clean, wash the food dishes between feeds and change the water pots daily. Cleaning the substrate will depend on the herptiles concerned.

For aquatic species, you will need to carry out partial water changes every three or four weeks. You can draw water from the tank either by baling or by using a length of plastic tubing as a siphon. In fact, there are several siphonic devices produced for aquarists that will make this job much quicker and more convenient. Basically these consist of a wide open-ended plastic tube, a plunger to create a flow of water and a length of plastic tube to lead the water to a suitable container. Once water is flowing out of the tank you can remove debris by stirring up the gravel with the open tube. Such regular maintenance is particularly

necessary with larger terrapins.
Always ensure that water added to the tank, either during a routine water change or to replace loss by evaporation, is at the same temperature as that already in the tank. Use a quick reacting alcohol thermometer to check the temperatures.

An undergravel filter (see page 28) should be able to keep the water clean in most aquatic vivariums and, once established, is relatively maintenance free. If you need extra filtration, the simplest type to use is an air-operated box filter, fitted either inside or on the outside of the tank. Box filters contain filter wool to trap solid particles and a layer of activated carbon granules to extract harmful chemicals from the water. You will need to clean and/or replace the filter mediums periodically, depending on the state of the vivarium.

For really messy aquatic herptiles, such as terrapins, you should consider fitting a power filter. This has an electrically driven pump

Right: *This simple siphonic device is ideal for cleaning the gravel in an aquatic vivarium without the need to empty the whole tank. Debris is whisked away in the flow of water set up by siphonic action.*

Above: *This is the standard way of carrying out a partial water change. Draw off and replace 20-25% of the water every three or four weeks.*

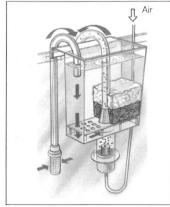

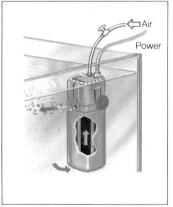

Above: *An air-operated box filter that fits on the outside of the tank. Water passes from the tank through the filter and back to the tank.*

Above: *This electrically driven power filter fits inside the tank and draws water in at the base. Air can be added to the outgoing stream.*

that draws water through a filter medium in the body of the unit. The most convenient power filters fit inside the tank in a vertical position. Water drawn in at the bottom of the unit passes through a replaceable filter cartridge and is pumped out at the top, at or just below the water level. Air can be added to the outgoing stream to freshen the water in the tank.

Summer quarters
During the warmer months of the year, you should be able to keep some herptiles out of doors. Tortoises have been kept in a state of semi-liberty for centuries, for example. Yet one of the problems of allowing tortoises to roam around a garden is that they can destroy prized plants in the process, either by eating them or by flattening them with their bulk. It is best to set aside an area of garden, preferably including a tiled area, for tortoises. A wall or small fence around the enclosure will prevent them

A basic outdoor run for hardy tortoises

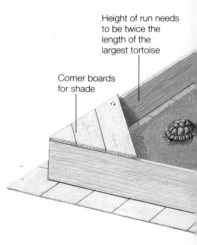

Height of run needs to be twice the length of the largest tortoise

Corner boards for shade

Use such an enclosure during warm dry weather, but take care that the tortoises cannot escape. Check them regularly in case one has fallen on its back – always a possibility.

escaping, providing it is taller than the longest tortoise, since some individuals can prove inveterate climbers. Always choose a relatively sunny location so the tortoises can follow the sun round during the course of the day. Provide some shade, though, and a suitable retreat where tortoises may retire during the warmest part of the day.

A greenhouse is ideal for accommodating tortoises overnight. Although you can leave tortoises outdoors on mild nights, there is always a risk that they might be attacked by foxes or develop a chill. You will also need to provide a suitable indoor area during periods of bad weather, enabling tortoises to continue eating and exercising. Install a heat lamp to provide warmth if required.

You can use a greenhouse as the summer quarters for other herptiles, where you can leave them to forage for food. Chameleons and tree frogs

fit into this category, although you will need to adapt the structure to prevent their escape. Cover open windows with muslin sheets, or, alternatively, partition off a small area of the greenhouse or conservatory for the purpose.

You can keep temperate amphibians and terrapins with a carapace longer than about 10cm (4in) in ponds during the summer, allowing them access to suitable areas of dry land. If space is limited, use a plastic moulded pond rimmed with marginal plants for terrapins. If you provide a suitable exit from the water, the terrapins will be able to bask on the marginal lip and yet be unable to climb out and escape.

Keep terrestrial amphibians in a cold frame, but never forget that they can escape through the smallest hole. Place such structures on level ground with no gaps beneath. The ideal location is a relatively dark corner, where direct sunlight will not cause overheating. Always include hiding places and a suitable area of water within the frame to complete the 'environment'.

Left: *Tropical species, such as these Red-footed Tortoises, need warm conditions, whether indoors or out.*

Corner boards to block climbers

Lift-off roof

Sliding door

Paving slab so that tortoise has access to a hard surface

Entrance ramp

Water bowl

Mount run on paving slabs to prevent tortoises escaping beneath

Feeding

At first, herptiles are likely to be nervous and may take a while to settle in their new enclosure before they show any interest in food. There is no need to worry unduly about this, providing the temperature is correct and you are offering the appropriate food. While some herptiles, such as tortoises and certain iguanas, are primarily vegetarian in their feeding habits, the majority tend to eat insects and other invertebrates. Some herptiles, notably snakes, will consume mammals. Here we look at a range of foods suitable for herptiles, beginning with the most commonly needed insects and invertebrates.

Insects and invertebrates

You can obtain a variety of suitable invertebrates from specialist suppliers in person or by mail order in the first instance and then establish your own cultures to provide a continuing supply. These are the principal live foods involved:

Crickets These have become very popular as a food item for many reptiles during recent years. Part of their popularity stems from the useful variation in their size. Hatchling crickets are only about 1-2mm (0.04-0.08in) in length and thus are ideal for small amphibians, whereas adult crickets at 15mm (0.6in) or so can be taken by large lizards. Do not house crickets of differing sizes together, however, since the smaller individuals are liable to be eaten by their elders. You can recognize female crickets by the long egglaying tube, or ovipositor, on the abdomen.

You can keep crickets in a simple covered aquarium. Offer them flour and similar foodstuffs, plus some fresh grass occasionally. A slice of apple is an ideal source of moisture, allowing the crickets to drink without the danger of drowning. You can breed them, although you will need to keep the commonly available strains at a relatively high temperature, around 27°C (81°F), for this purpose. The eggs are laid on the floor of the container in sand and hatch within about 21 days.

Mealworms In spite of the name, these are not worms, but the larval stage in the life cycle of the Flour Beetle (*Tenebrio molitor*). In terms of their nutritive value, they tend to be low in calcium; the addition of sterilized bone flour to their feed can help to counteract this deficiency. They are widely used as a live food for herptiles, but they do possess a hard outer covering of chitin that is relatively indigestible. Various sizes of mealworm are available, but their care is essentially the same. You can maintain them perfectly well in a plastic ice-cream container. Punch small holes in the lid and line the container with a thick layer of chicken meal. Place a piece of apple (and replace as necessary) on the surface to act as a source of moisture.

It is not difficult to breed mealworms. The adult beetles lay eggs that hatch within about six weeks. Start cultures in sequence to ensure a regular source of larvae. Do not use mealworms as the sole food for insectivorous herptiles, however, because of their poor calcium content.

Below: *Mealworms are a popular food for herptiles, but they do not provide a balanced diet on their own.*

Flies While all stages in the life cycle of flies can be valuable for feeding to herptiles, breeding these insects is not a pleasant occupation. You can buy larvae from fishing bait suppliers, but avoid dyed maggots in case they prove toxic. In view of their unsavoury feeding habits there is a possibility that maggots could transmit *Salmonella* bacteria to herptiles (see page 58). Ideally, 'clean' maggots for several days in a container lined with bran. If you keep them at room temperature, the larvae will pupate and soon emerge as adult flies. You can offer these to various lizards, such as chameleons. If you house adult flies in muslin cages, you can channel batches through an exit directly into the vivarium.

If you want to culture flies, any offal placed outside in a suitable container during the summer will attract them. They will lay small clusters of eggs that may hatch in only a day or so. The maggots will then continue to feed on the putrifying remains of their immediate environment. Their rapid life cycle and high potential yield can make flies a relatively cheap source of live food for many herptiles.

Fruit flies (*Drosophila*) These tiny flies are not substantial enough to be of value in feeding large lizards, but they are useful for small amphibians, in particular. They are widely used in laboratories for genetical research purposes, and a strain with vestigial wings has been produced. These are particularly valuable as food, since not only are they easier prey but they are also less likely to escape from the confines of the vivarium.

You will need to buy these 'wingless' fruit flies in the first instance, but you can obtain the normal type simply by leaving some ripe fruit out of doors in a jar during warm weather. Banana skins are ideal, since they will not smell or grow moulds to the same extent as other fruits. The flies will lay their eggs on the fruit and once you can see the tiny larvae, cover the jar with a muslin. Set up several such cultures in succession to ensure a continuous supply.

To feed them to your amphibians, place the jar in the vivarium and cut a small hole in the muslin. This will enable the flies to escape, but prevent the amphibians disturbing

Below: *Cultures of fruit flies, an ideal food for small amphibians, can be raised easily in warm conditions.*

the culture. To keep a supply going during the winter, maintain the jars at a temperature of around 23°C (73°F). You can use supplementary sugar-based foods, but banana skins alone will sustain fruit flies quite successfully.

Whiteworms Colonies of these small, threadlike worms are very useful for feeding amphibians and small reptiles, including hatchling terrapins. Ask a specialist live food dealer or aquarist store to provide a starter colony. Divide this into groups and bury each portion under a substrate of damp peat in separate margarine tubs or similar containers. Place pieces of brown bread moistened with milk in the peat and the worms will cluster around these to feed. Be sure to change the food regularly before it becomes sour. Punch holes in the lid of the container for ventilation. It will take a month or so, at a temperature of 20°C (68°F) for the colonies to become established. Then you can remove the worms with forceps or separate them from the food in a saucer of water. Other even smaller worms, such as microworms and grindalworms, are

Above: *Whiteworms can be cultured in a ventilated container of moist peat with pieces of bread as food.*
Below: *Separate the worms from the peat and food in a saucer of water.*

also sold as cultures; you can raise them in the same way as that recommended for whiteworms.

Redworms and earthworms
Redworms are generally smaller than earthworms and prove a useful stand-by, since they are a popular fishing bait and thus widely available. Most amphibians and certain reptiles, such as Box Tortoises, will readily take redworms and earthworms. If you have a garden, you can simply dig earthworms out of the soil. Laying a well-watered piece of hessian sacking on the soil surface should attract worms, particularly if there is some vegetable matter underneath it. Keep them in damp surroundings, such as an old margarine tub filled with grass, so that they empty their intestines before you use them as food. You may find it more convenient, particularly during the winter when the ground is frozen, to buy earthworms or redworms. Mail order suppliers of live food advertise in the columns of both fishkeeping and avicultural publications.

You can gather a variety of other live foods in a garden, provided no insecticides have been used. Dragging a net through long grass will produce a host of useful creatures. Spiders are particularly appreciated by most herptiles, for example, and greenfly are suitable for many amphibians. Even garden snails may be accepted by some herptiles, which they eat complete with the shell – a valuable source of minerals.

Aquatic invertebrates
Aquatic invertebrates are only useful for feeding to aquatic herptiles and even then there are disease risks associated with using them that may encourage you to consider other options, such as whiteworm. The main types of aquatic live food available are *Tubifex* worms and *Daphnia*.

Tubifex These tiny reddish worms congregate in slime around such unsavoury places as sewage outlets. Although thoroughly

Above: *Tubifex worms are eaten readily by many aquatic herptiles. Wash them thoroughly before use.*

washed before sale, they can prove a source of disease. Keep *Tubifex* in a cool spot and change the water regularly if you want to keep the worms alive for any length of time. A flattish container, such as a cat-litter tray, placed under a dripping tap is ideal. *Tubifex* worms are particularly relished by young terrapins and aquatic frogs and toads.

Daphnia These minute crustaceans are commonly known as water fleas simply because of their shape. They live in still fresh water, such as ponds. You can buy them in plastic bags full of water. The supplier normally keeps them under refrigeration, and it is worth checking that a significant proportion of the *Daphnia* are alive before you buy a batch. In order to avoid emptying the water from the bag directly into the tank, pour the water away through a muslin net and rinse the *Daphnia*-filled net in the tank water.

Supplies of fresh *Tubifex* and *Daphnia* are not always reliable and certainly a whiteworm culture will be useful to counter any shortfall. Another option is to buy prepared live foods that are guaranteed free from disease. A range of these gamma-irradiated products are

available, including *Tubifex*, bloodworm and lancefish. These are supplemented with vitamins and help to provide a balanced diet. Keep the packs deep frozen and break off and thaw pieces when you need them.

Amphibians, particularly, are attracted to their prey by its movement, which can be a problem, but if you wave pieces of these products around gently in the water you should be able to encourage the animals to eat. Fix a chunk firmly to a piece of string (but ensure that the string will not be accidentally ingested) or on the end of a blunt matchstick. Terrapins usually present no problems; they will quickly become accustomed to taking inert foods.

Rodents
The vast majority of snakes are dependent on mammals – particularly rodents – to form the basis of their diet. Under normal circumstances, however, you should not need to offer living rodents. Indeed, this may well prove positively dangerous to the snakes, since both rats and mice may bite and cause serious if not fatal injuries with their sharp teeth.

If you want to keep rodents for feeding purposes, house them in secure escape-proof containers. Apart from the risk of colonies becoming established in the house, escaping rodents may savage reptiles housed in adjoining accommodation. Using plastic containers and changing the bedding regularly will help to reduce the smell associated with keeping rodents. Mature female mice cycle every five days and produce a litter of up to eight offspring after a gestation period of three weeks. The most humane method of killing young mice is to adminster a sharp blow to the back of the head. Alternatively, place one in a dry aquarium containing a metal trap, which should break the animal's neck instantaneously.

You do not need to keep a colony of rodents in order to feed a snake, since you can buy dead rodents of various sizes in a deep-frozen state from herpetological suppliers. Make enquiries about a local source when you buy your snake. You will need to thaw frozen rodents out very carefully to ensure that there are no ice crystals remaining in their bodies before you use them. Day-old mice, known as pinkies, are generally recommended for smaller snakes and other herptiles, including monitor lizards and giant toads. If your snake is not used to taking dead prey, wave a rodent about on a feeding stick to encourage it to strike at the food.

The sense of smell is very important to many herptiles when assessing potential food, and you can apply an appetising scent to improve the food's palatability. Rat snakes, for example, may refuse rats if they are used to mice; rubbing a dead mouse around the head of a dead rat tranfers the scent and makes the rat palatable to the snake. And you can persuade young garter snakes to take fish by mixing it with earthworms, which they feed on after hatching.

Offering the whole carcass minimizes the risk of nutritional deficiencies occurring, which is inevitable if you feed only selected parts of the carcass on a regular basis without any supplement. Minced meat used as terrapin food illustrates this point very well, since it is low in Vitamin A and has a calcium:phosphorus ratio of the order of 1:20. The lack of Vitamin A ultimately causes blindness and death, and the imbalance in essential minerals causes shell deformity (see page 54).

Day-old chicks, surplus to a hatchery's requirements, are also valuable as reptile food in a similar way to rodents. They are supplied dead and are thus easy to handle.

Feeding herbivorous herptiles
It may seem at first sight that herbivorous herptiles are relatively

Below: *A young Burmese Python feeds on a chick. The diet of the young may differ from the adults.*

easy to cater for, but this is not necessarily the case. They need a suitably varied diet and yet there is a considerable diversity in the nutritive values of plants used for feeding purposes. Although it is freely available, avoid using lettuce if possible; it consists of little more than water and appears to have an addictive quality, particularly for tortoises. Cabbage, with its depressant effect on thyroid activity, is also best avoided as a major ingredient of the diet.

Greenfoods that are of particular value are dandelion leaves, cress and parsley. They are relatively high in protein and carbohydrate, as well as being rich in essential vitamins and minerals. You can cultivate these plants very easily, and growing cress and parsley indoors will give you a year-round supply.

The fibre content of the diet is important, certainly in the case of tortoises, and a lack of fibre can drive certain individuals to consume stones. A shortage of fibre may delay passage of food through the gut and can cause persistent diarrhoea. Dandelion leaves, cress and parsley all have relatively high levels of fibre, compared with both lettuce and cabbage.

Some tortoises are more inclined

Above: Predominantly herbivorous reptiles, such as these tortoises, eat relatively large quantities of food; always feed them accordingly.

to eat fruit, notably forest species such as the Red-footed Tortoise. Plums form part of their natural diet in the wild, and you can supplement this out of season with other items, such as tomatoes. These are usually available throughout the year, and you can also stock up the freezer when cheap bulk supplies are plentiful. Tomatoes are especially valuable for tortoises emerging from hibernation; they have a relatively high water content and help to encourage the reptiles to start eating again.

It is doubtful if any herptile is totally vegetarian in its feeding habits, and items such as hard-boiled egg, a complete cat food or even soaked mynah bird pellets will all be accepted by individuals. Certain components of protein, known as essential amino-acid residues, are supplied by foods of this nature.

Frequency of feeding
The frequency of feeding depends upon the herptile concerned and its age; young individuals have

correspondingly greater appetites. As a general rule, feed amphibians every day, taking care to offer no more food than they will consume within a short space of time. Also feed chelonians and small lizards on a daily basis, although they can go for considerable periods without food and show no obvious ill-effects at first. Herbivorous reptiles have relatively large appetites, and so need a considerable intake of food to satisfy their requirements.

One of the significant problems of keeping reptiles in good health in captivity is obesity. Snakes, with their very efficient digestive systems, need feeding in most cases only once a week. One novel means of encouraging activity among snakes in zoos is to house them in the company of large tortoises. The idea is that the tortoises will cause the snake to move and thus expend energy, rather than just remaining inactive in one spot. You must make every effort to maintain your herptiles in good condition and modify their food intake if necessary to prevent them from becoming obese. Obese herptiles have reduced reproductive activity and may die sooner than their slimmer counterparts.

You will need to supervise the feeding of certain herptiles. Terrapins, especially, should have a separate feeding tank, where you can transfer them at feeding times. This not only enables you to keep a check on individual appetites, but also helps to prevent unnecessary soiling of the water in their main vivarium. Although you can house large terrapins safely alongside smaller individuals, never feed them simultaneously, since injuries can result at this time. Snakes may even consume each other, particularly when food is offered, so do not keep hatchlings with adults. Certain species tend to be more cannibalistic than others, with King Snakes being noted offenders in this regard.

Always provide a supply of water in the vivarium, even for herptiles that appear to drink very little. If nothing else, it will help to maintain the humidity, which can prove vital in ensuring that the creatures remain healthy. Geckos, for

A basic feeding guide for the major groups of herptiles

▼ ANIMALS / FOODS ▶	INSECTS eg: Crickets, Mealworms, Flies, Fruit flies	WORMS eg: Redworms, Earthworms, Whiteworms, Grindalworms	AQUATIC INVERTEBRATES eg: Daphnia, Tubifex	DEEP FROZEN INVERTEBRATES eg: Tubifex, Bloodworm, Lancefish	UNSPECIFIED MEAT...
TORTOISES, TURTLES AND TERRAPINS	(Mealworms in some cases)	Box Tortoises Turtles Terrapins	(Tubifex)	Not tortoises	Not tortoi...
CROCODILES, CAIMANS AND ALLIGATORS					
LIZARDS					Monitors
SNAKES	Hatchlings may take large items of this type				
FROGS AND TOADS				If moving	
NEWTS AND SALAMANDERS				If moving	

example, are likely to encounter difficulty in shedding their skins in a dry atmosphere. If skin builds up on their specialized toes this can interfere with the blood supply and cause loss of digits.

The depth of the water container will depend on the creatures themselves, since there must be no risk of them drowning or becoming trapped. Use a solid ceramic bowl; this is less likely to be tipped up, possibly causing injury. You may need to bury the bowl in the substrate so that the rim of the container does not present a barrier to the water within. Some species, notably the water snakes and Box Tortoises, will immerse themselves in a container of water, yet they must also have access to a dry surrounding area. Certain reptiles, particularly chameleons, will not drink from a container. For these you will need to spray the vivarium regularly so that they can obtain essential moisture from the droplets alighting on any plants or suitable surfaces.

It is a good idea to provide a vitamin and mineral supplement on a regular basis. Supplements prepared especially for reptiles and amphibians are widely available. You can also use general products of this type, but always check that they contain Vitamin D in the form of D_3 rather than as D_2. (Vitamin D_2 is more commonly included in preparations marketed for dogs, cats and small mammals.) It is difficult to recommend precise dosages of supplements; dusting the food once or twice a week is likely to be adequate in most cases. Powder is the most convenient form since it will readily adhere to moist surfaces, such as cut fruit or wet leaves. Liquid preparations may be more difficult to administer, although you can give them directly by mouth when required.

Below: *This table summarises the feeding habits of the main groups of herptiles. Try to give your herptiles a varied diet over a period of time to keep them in good health. Provide vitamin and mineral supplements to help correct any dietary shortages of these essential chemicals. Detailed feeding advice is given in Part Two.*

VEGETABLE FOODS FRUIT	SMALL WHOLE MAMMALS eg: Pinkies (Day-old mice) Day-old chicks	LARGER WHOLE MAMMALS eg: Older mice, Chickens, Rabbits	SNAILS, SLUGS	AMPHIBIANS	EGGS	FISH
...rtoises and ...x Turtles ...pecially			Box Tortoises	Aquatic species		Aquatic species
	Feed predominantly on these foods					
	Tegus Larger geckos Monitors		Slow Worm		Monitors	
	Feed predominantly on these foods		Possibly	Water Snakes Grass Snakes Garter Snakes	Egg-eating Snake	Water Snakes Grass Snakes Garter Snakes
...dpoles may ...ke plant ...atter	Giant Toad Bullfrog		Possibly	Can be cannibalistic		Possibly
			Possibly			Possibly

Breeding herptiles

Interest in breeding herptiles has grown considerably over recent years, and a greater understanding of their reproductive needs has led to more consistent results. Success is not without its problems, however. The reproductive capacity of amphibians in particular is immense; some frogs may produce as many as 30,000 eggs. Clearly, rearing only a fraction of these successfully demands substantial extra accommodation.

Sexing

Distinguishing between male and female in many herptiles is not an easy process. The following guidelines may help you to pair up herptiles, although some of the distinctions may only be apparent during the breeding season. They are not necessarily reliable in young herptiles, however. And just to confuse the issue, the age of maturity varies considerably, being often more a reflection of size rather than of age. Since most captive-reared herptiles grow faster than their wild counterparts, they breed at a correspondingly earlier age.

In chelonians, male tortoises have more concave plastrons than females and, in some instances, longer tails. In aquatic turtles, the claws on the front feet of males grow very long, apparently to help them grip the females during mating, which takes place in water.

Male lizards usually have enhanced colour and head ornamentations compared to females and they also have more evident pores in front of the anus, extending across both hind limbs. This region is equally significant in sexing newts and salamanders, since the edges of the anus are more swollen in males. In addition, at the onset of the breeding period, males often become brighter and develop crests, while females swell with eggs. A similar change occurs in anurans; the males develop swellings – nuptial pads – on their forelegs and become increasingly vocal. The tail (i.e. the region of the body behind the cloaca) provides a means of sexing snakes; it is invariably longer in males, which may also show a slight enlargement behind the cloacal opening.

Since these methods are not reliable in every case, it may be necessary to carry out an internal examination in order to establish the sex of an individual. Special probes are marketed for use in snakes and various lizards. The technique involves inserting a solid probe of appropriate size into and backwards behind the vent. In females the probe can be inserted for a much greater distance than in males, where the presence of the reproductive organs – the hemipenes – restricts passage of the probe. It is possible, therefore, to judge the sex of the animal by seeing how far the probe can be

Below: *Femoral pores such as these serve to distinguish male lizards from their female counterparts.*

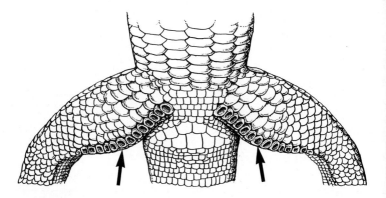

Above: *A pair of Mediterranean Spur-thighed Tortoises. The male is on the left, with a concave plastron and longer tail than the female.*

inserted. This means of examination must be undertaken very carefully with adequate lubrication applied to the probe; it is very easy to injure a reptile internally, ruining the possibility of successful breeding and possibly even killing it in the process. If you have any doubt about using this method, seek expert advice and assistance. Another technique – laparotomy sexing – entails direct viewing of the sex organs with an endoscope while

Below: *There is a clear difference in the cloacal region between male (top) and female (bottom) newts.*

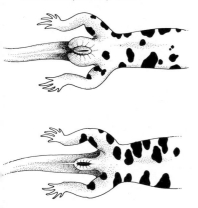

the animal is anaesthetized.

Even blood tests may be necessary in some cases to help establish the sex of individual herptiles. Laboratory tests on a blood sample can reveal the relative levels of the male hormone, testosterone. This method may not be conclusive, however, for the level of testosterone varies during the year and the results from immature animals may prove misleading.

Breeding stimuli
A number of different factors appear to stimulate breeding activity in herptiles. Studies show that temperature is vitally important in the wild. In Box Tortoises, for example, 17°C (63°F) is a crucial temperature in reproductive terms. Above this figure, sperm production in males begins in earnest and, during spring, the females start ovulating. A period of relatively low temperature can also act as a 'trigger' to reproductive activity. Transferring temperate amphibians to a refrigerator for a week or so at a temperature of 5°C (41°F) mimics the normal hibernation process and stimulates them to breed when they are returned to warmer conditions.

As you would expect, the importance of hibernation is greatest in herptiles from temperate climates. Yet a number of reports suggest that a temperature fall can also stimulate breeding in reptiles from tropical areas. The successful breeding of the white-throated subspecies of the Bosc's Monitor at Rotterdam Zoo illustrates this point. When the heating system failed, these lizards were exposed to a maximum temperature of 18°C (64°F) over a period of eight days. Within two days of the temperature being raised again to a daytime minimum of 25°C (77°F) mating was observed. A similar case in California involved various species of *Liasis* python, with copulation being noted once the power was restored. There is an associated risk, however, that respiratory infection may follow such a drastic alteration in the herptile's environmental conditions.

Although the level of humidity is certainly vital when it comes to successful hatching of eggs under captive conditions, its importance in the wild is unclear. It is known that the breeding cycles of various species are linked with periods of rainfall, but this may simply be because the water softens the ground and facilitates nesting.

The sex ratio can also prove significant, since many amphibians and reptiles congregate for breeding purposes. To encourage mating in *Thamnophis*, for example, you should house several males with a single female. Yet conversely, evidence suggests that overcrowding lizards will cause a decrease in reproductive activity and the males will fight among themselves.

Mating

As in many groups of animals, the sense of smell in herptiles can assume great importance as a preliminary to mating. The reddish tinge that develops on the Elongated Tortoise's forehead during the breeding season, for example, is thought to reflect the increased blood flow to the olfactory region. (See entry on page 66.) And many female chelonians almost certainly produce pheromones (enticing biological 'scents' that attract mates when they are sexually active).

Before mating, males may display to their intended mates. This behaviour is particularly evident among lizards.

Mating itself can be a violent encounter. In chelonians, for example, the male repeatedly attempts to bite and batter an intended female. It may appear as though she is being attacked, but few, if any, signs of injury are ever apparent. Some herptiles will mate

Below: *Many reptiles live solitary lives, congregating only for breeding purposes. In tortoises, mating can be a fairly violent activity.*

Above: *A pair of frogs mating in a mass of spawn. The large numbers of eggs produced by the female are fertilized externally by the male.*

several times a day over the course of several weeks if the opportunity permits, or copulation can be a single encounter. Indeed, in some cases, there is no direct contact between the partners. In newts, for instance, the spermatozoa are enclosed in a special capsule – the spermatophore – which the female grasps and transfers to her cloaca, thus fertilizing the eggs inside her body. In some instances, the spermatophore is taken up directly into the cloaca.

Anurans remain in close physical contact throughout the mating process, with the male holding his mate in a characteristic grip known as the amplexus. As the eggs are laid, the male fertilizes them externally and they swell on contact with water.

By contrast, only one mating appears to be necessary in certain reptiles for them to produce fertile eggs for a number of seasons. The mechanism of sperm storage within the female reproductive tract is unclear, but in some cases the spermatozoa may remain viable for several years. A mature female chelonian, housed on her own, for example, is quite capable of laying fertile eggs, although the level of fertility declines quite sharply as the years pass.

Nesting and egg laying
Most herptiles reproduce by means of eggs and are described as oviparous, although there are exceptions – the boas, for example – which give birth to live young.

To encourage successful nesting and egg laying, you should provide a breeding environment that reflects the needs of the individual species concerned. For example, geckos lay a pair of eggs in a suitably concealed place in the vivarium whereas others, such as iguanas, may bury their eggs. Clearly, herptiles that bury their eggs can present problems in the vivarium, where the depth of the substrate may not allow them to excavate a suitably deep nesting chamber. Should the eggs be scattered over the surface, there is always the danger that they will be broken or even eaten.

You can make an acceptable nesting site for many herptiles by filling a half-litre ice-cream container with a mixture of damp peat and sand. If you keep the surface moist the female will be attracted by the moisture and lay her eggs in the container. In snakes and most lizards, the relatively soft-shelled eggs will swell on contact with moisture. A female with eggs appears relatively swollen. A sudden apparent loss of weight and signs that the substrate has been disturbed suggest that egg laying has taken place. You can confirm this by cautiously examining the container.

Chelonians present more problems when it comes to obtaining their eggs. Deprived of a suitable locality, terrapins may lay in the water or break their eggs on land. To suit terrapins, therefore, fit the container at floor level in the basking area of their tank. Adopt a similar approach for tortoises housed indoors, although you may need to raise the whole floor of the vivarium to accommodate the nesting container.

Above: *Some snakes produce live young, but others – such as the Burmese Python here – lay eggs.*

If you keep tortoises outdoors, ranging over part of the garden, you may find it difficult to recognize a nesting site. Doubtless, many clutches of eggs are lost for this reason. Since excavating a nesting site is a protracted process, lasting forty minutes or so, and often takes place during the latter part of the afternoon, it should be possible to detect the site before the operation is complete. Unfortunately, the female is so adept at covering her tracks that this is not necessarily so. At least you can begin your search on the premise that a damp spot in the enclosure may be attractive for egg laying.

In the majority of cases, female herptiles will ignore their eggs once they have been laid. There are exceptions; the Brown Tortoise (*Testudo emys*), an Asian species, actually guards her domed nest, butting any creatures that approach. And female pythons stay with their clutches, not feeding throughout the incubation period and remaining wrapped around the eggs until they hatch.

Setting up a spawning tank for amphibians depends on the species concerned. Plants can be important; newts, for example, lay their eggs on the undersurfaces of leaves, which they then curl up to hide their location. Generally, after spawning has taken place, you should transfer the adults to separate quarters, leaving the eggs to develop on their own. Eggs that

were not fertilized rapidly turn white as they become attacked by fungus. You can remove them if required, but the infection does not usually spread to healthy eggs.

Incubation

While pythons can be left with their eggs under vivarium conditions, it is advisable to remove the eggs of other herptiles carefully and incubate them separately. Do this as soon as possible, and once the eggs are in the incubator, leave them undisturbed; studies on tortoise eggs show that their hatchability is compromised if they are moved within days of laying. You do not need to turn reptile eggs, unlike birds' eggs. Mark the top of the eggs with a pencil while they are still in the nesting chamber and set the eggs with this surface uppermost in the incubator.

No sophisticated equipment is required to incubate most reptile eggs successfully. To maintain the temperature and humidity at the required level, a tank covered with a vivarium lid and heated by an ordinary light bulb will usually suffice for incubation.

If the reptile has laid in a nesting container, transfer the substrate and the eggs together to the incubator. If you need to transfer the eggs alone, set them on a bed of peat and do not bury them. If the parchment-shelled eggs produced by snakes and some lizards begin to shrivel, this is a sign that the level of humidity is too low. Spraying the surrounding substrate lightly with tepid water will enable moisture to enter through the egg shell. Ideally, maintain the relative humidity in the incubator at about 75-80 percent. Keep a check on the humidity level using a hygrometer, a cheap and simple device commonly sold in gardening stores. Placing a pot of water in the incubator should help to maintain the humidity.

Incubation can take 10 weeks or longer, depending on the species and the temperature in the incubator. During this period, the shells may become discoloured or develop areas of mould on them. This is natural and should not have a harmful effect on hatching. Reptile eggs seem to possess a natural defence mechanism that restricts fungal development, even in conditions that normally favour the growth of such microorganisms.

Below: A simple incubator for reptile eggs. Check the humidity daily and keep a spare light bulb in case a replacement is needed urgently.

Indeed, reptile eggs appear quite resilient under certain circumstances; there is a reliable record of Box Tortoise eggs hatching successfully after being immersed in water for two days.

If you are really serious about breeding reptiles, you should consider obtaining an incubator that can be set to operate within a very fine temperature range. A range of small incubators, marketed essentially for hatching parrots and other birds in the domestic environment, are suitable for hatching reptile eggs, although it may be difficult to bring the temperature down to the relatively low level required. Always check on this point before you buy a particular model. There is no need to consider the expense of an automatic turning system, since the eggs should be left alone once they are in place. Never position the incubator in direct sunlight; this can effectively cook the eggs within the dome.

Temperature and sex ratio
Temperature can influence more than the length of incubation. Recent studies have confirmed that there can be a direct link between the temperature at which the eggs

A basic incubator

Light bulb or infrared heater connected to thermostat

Vivarium lid

Eggs set on peat in container

Hygrometer to register humidity

Water dish beneath heat source to provide humidity. Keep filled

Thermometer near heat source to monitor temperature

are incubated and the sex of the hatchlings. Clearly, being able to manipulate the sex ratio is potentially very important in breeding endangered species, for example.

In many animals, particularly mammals and birds, the sex of the organism is determined by sex chromosomes in its genetic make-up. In reptiles the situation is rather confused. Many snakes and lizards possess sex chromosomes, as do members of the terrapin family Kinosternidae. Yet in other cases, where sex chromosomes are absent, the sex of the individual is determined during the incubation period by the local environmental temperature. At a relatively low temperature, offspring of one sex are produced, and at a slightly higher temperature, both sexes are produced. Finally, above a certain temperature threshold, youngsters of the other sex can be anticipated.

A classic example of this general rule is provided by the Painted Turtle. Males are produced at 28°C (82°F), both sexes at 29°C (84°F) and females at 30°C (86°F). The crucial phase appears to be in the middle of the incubation period, when the sex organs are developing in the body. Many other chelonians also produce females at the highest incubation temperature, although

Below: *How incubation temperature affects offspring sex in the Painted Turtle. Research shows that different results can occur in other species.*

this is species dependent. In the Snapping Turtle, for example, females predominate in the hatchlings above and below the temperature range 22-28°C (72-82°F). And in *Trionyx* turtles, incubation temperature does not appear to influence the sex of the offspring at all.

In lizards, a reverse situation applies: males predominate at the highest temperature. It may be that temperature alone is not the only factor involved, since the latest research suggests that humidity may also influence the sex of the hatchlings. No firm evidence to support this view is yet available, but studies being undertaken by Dr Jim Bull at the University of Texas, USA and other workers are continuing and a clearer picture may soon emerge.

Hatching and rearing
The first sign of hatching is likely to be a crack in the shell, made by the young reptile's egg-tooth. This projection on the snout soon disappears, having served its purpose once the reptile emerges from the egg. Following the appearance of the initial crack, it may take several days for the hatchling to finally break free of the shell. This need not give cause for concern; there is no risk that the young reptile will starve to death, because it has ample reserves of food still present in its yolk sac. This may persist as a swelling on the underside of the body for a short

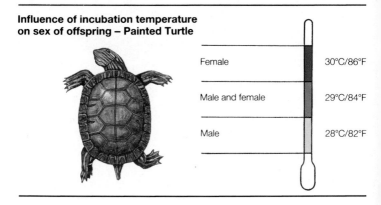

Influence of incubation temperature on sex of offspring – Painted Turtle

Female	30°C/86°F
Male and female	29°C/84°F
Male	28°C/82°F

Above: *A Black Rat Snake emerging from its egg. At first, it will survive on the remains of its yolk sac and then start to feed on its own. Offer pinkies (day-old mice) as a first food.*

period until it is fully absorbed, when the dry membrane remaining will drop off. Always keep newly hatched reptiles on clean bedding, however, to minimize the risk of any yolk sac infection and possible septicaemia (see page 57).

If there appears to be no movement for about 48 hours after the first crack has developed, then carefully open part of the shell from the site of the crack. Once the reptile has fully emerged, provide suitable food and water within easy reach – although it may well not eat for several days or so. Ensure that the food is compatible with the size of the youngster; hatchling crickets and fruit flies are particularly valuable for insectivorous creatures at this time. Certain snakes, such as the King Snakes, can prove especially difficult to rear because of their small size. You may need to cut up pinkies and force feed the youngsters for several months in some instances. Herbivorous reptiles, such as Green Iguanas, will take more insects and animal food when they are young, as their protein requirement is higher.

Providing a varied selection of foods at this stage ensures that they develop a sound skeletal structure.

The length of time taken for young tadpoles to emerge is variable, depending upon the species concerned and to some extent on the water temperature. Be sure to allow tadpoles adequate space as they develop, otherwise losses are likely to occur. Various rearing foods are widely available. Fish foods used for rearing fry, small water fleas and microworms are all suitable at first. As the tadpoles grow, supplement the diet with larger items, such as irradiated frozen *Tubifex* worms, thawed and cut into pieces. Always offer small quantities several times a day to avoid polluting the water with uneaten food.

As their life cycle advances, you will see the tadpoles change. The hind legs invariably develop first, followed by the front limbs, as the tail gradually shrinks in size. At the same time as the legs begin to appear, the gills are gradually replaced by lungs. Be sure to provide some means for the developing adults to leave the water. Several months will elapse before the young frogs and toads are able to live on land, and possibly three years or so before they are able to breed.

Health care

Health problems are most likely to arise in newly-acquired herptiles, and for this reason, always keep new arrivals separate from established stock. Signs of illness will depend to some extent on the disease concerned, but general indicators of malaise can also be apparent. Snakes, for example, may not shed their skins fully, with the so-called spectacles being retained over the eyes, giving a whitish glaze. If this should happen, soak the spectacles off very gently, to avoid damaging the cornea beneath.

Many of the ailments that may afflict your herptiles require skilled veterinary attention. While not all veterinarians possess specialized knowledge of herptiles, they can, if necessary, refer a case to a more experienced colleague. You may find it worthwhile to enquire locally which veterinarian is consulted by other herptile owners.

Poor appetite

Poor appetite may be associated with ill-health or it may reflect natural behaviour. Royal Pythons, for example, will not normally feed during their breeding season, which extends over several months. Similarly, Bosc's Monitors fast naturally for nearly six months in the Sahelian part of their natural range, so studies in Senegal have revealed.

Under normal circumstances, you should make every effort to entice a herptile to eat. It may be that bullying is responsible for an apparent lack of appetite; in a group of lizards with a well-defined social structure, for example, the weaker individuals may be harassed and prevented from feeding. Providing incorrect food, such as offering large crickets to small anurans, can also be responsible for a herptile's refusal to eat. And a low vivarium temperature will often serve to depress feeding activity. Dehydration can also be significant; tortoises emerging from hibernation may not feed until they have drunk well. Indeed, a tortoise that refuses to eat should be immersed in a bath of warm water up to the level of its mouth. No chelonian with blocked

nostrils and closed eyes is likely to feed, and bathing is a vital part of nursing care to maximise the chances of a recovery.

Mouth rot One of the most common infectious reasons for lack of appetite is often described as 'mouth rot', or necrotic stomatitis. It is prevalent in terrestrial chelonians and snakes, often being associated with a foul odour around the head in severe cases. Early signs are whitish areas, with a furry appearance, on the surface of the tongue or at the sides of the mouth. Within a few days the spots will coalesce, covering the inside of the mouth and even spreading down the throat.

There is no single causal microorganism for mouth rot, although bacteria of the Gram-negative group – notably *Pseudomonas* – are often isolated. Treatment with antibiotics needs to begin as soon as possible; you can dust powder inside the mouth, and an injection administered by a veterinarian is also to be recommended in more advanced cases. This is important because although the mouth may start to heal successfully using the powder alone, pieces of the infective debris are liable to break off and be swallowed. They can then cause an infection lower down the digestive

Above: *The sunken and closed eyes of a dehydrated tortoise. Fluid lost during hibernation must be replaced.*

tract, in the gut itself, and an injection of an appropriate antibiotic should help to prevent this forming.

If possible, use forceps to gently lift off pieces of the material as signs of healing become apparent. Simply pulling off debris is liable to lead to serious bleeding, since the underlying tissue is invaded by the bacteria responsible. A general vitamin product can be valuable at this time. There is some evidence to suggest that a deficiency of Vitamin C may make herptiles susceptible to infections of this type, while Vitamin A is always useful in assisting the creature's response to infection.

Opening a reptile's mouth, in order to look inside or treat it, can prove difficult. Preferably, ask someone else to hold the animal so that you can concentrate exclusively on the mouth. The first step, at least with chelonians, is to restrain the head firmly and then prize the jaws apart, holding the upper jaw firmly and pushing the lower jaw down. Some substances may encourage a chelonian to open its mouth, so that you can insert a stout matchstick or similar gag between the jaws. Olive oil is effective for terrapins and blackcurrant jelly may do the trick in some tortoises. Smear these substances around the jaws, particularly where they are in contact.

While in many cases necrotic stomatitis may reflect a poor overall state of health, trauma and injury around the head can also lay an animal open to infections of this type. Snakes and certain lizards, notably monitors, may persist in rubbing their heads on the glass at the front of the vivarium, seeking a way out. This behaviour is most

Below: *The characteristic appearance of mouth rot in a tortoise. It may be seen on emergence from hibernation. Treat it promptly.*

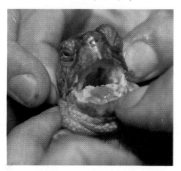

Below: *Measure the shell length of your tortoise, weigh it and check against this graph (based on the work of Dr. O. F. Jackson). If it is below average, do not hibernate it but feed it well over the winter months.*

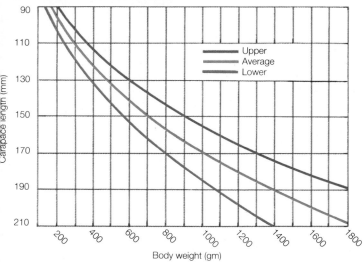

likely when you first acquire the animals and particularly so if there is little accessible cover in the vivarium where they could retreat. If you allow it to continue unchecked, such behaviour will ultimately lead to superficial injury and infection around the mouth, which can spread within. Tape a broad band of paper around the base of the vivarium glass to reduce such reactions, before damage results.

Dietary disorders
In herptiles that do eat freely, problems can arise if you offer them an unsuitable diet. This applies especially to terrapins. For example, never feed just raw red meat to any of the carnivorous herptiles. It is low in Vitamin A and calcium and cannot in any sense be regarded as an ideal diet, even if the meat is best steak! The key is variety – too much raw fish can be equally harmful, since the enzyme thiaminase present in the body tissues of the fish will destroy Vitamin B_1 in the herptile.

Vitamins A and D_3 are especially significant for reptiles. These fat-soluble vitamins are stored in the liver, so deficiencies will not become apparent immediately, but they can rapidly prove fatal once the signs appear. Red-eared Sliders/Terrapins and Box Tortoises are particularly at risk.

Vitamin A deficiency The first signs of Vitamin A deficiency are that the eyelids become swollen and stuck together. Deprived of its sight, the affected reptile then refuses to eat. The eyes themselves are unaffected; it is the swelling of the Harderian glands around the eyes that causes these symptoms. Subsequently, other changes occur in the body, giving rise to kidney damage and, terminally, swelling around the feet known as oedema.

If you discover these symptoms at an early stage, it is quite possible to ensure a full recovery. An injection of Vitamin A (carried out by a veterinarian) coupled with bathing of the eyes can lead to a spectacular improvement. You can also give the vitamin orally in a liquid preparation.

Above: *The first signs of Vitamin A deficiency may be swollen eyes. Here, the nostrils are also blocked. With treatment animals recover.*

Always take care that there is no risk of the reptile choking, however; just a few drops several times a day will help to speed recovery.

When the eyes are closed, there is often a discharge from the nostrils, because of the connection between the eyes and nose. Once the eyes open, tear fluid is able to wash over the surfaces as normal and this discharge will normally clear up. In some cases, however, such discharges are much more serious and indicate a respiratory infection.

Vitamin D_3 and calcium Failure to provide sufficient Vitamin D_3 and calcium and phosphorous in the correct ratio of 1:1 may cause soft shells in chelonians, as well as weak bones and flabby limbs. Such deficiencies may be environmental or dietary in origin. Reptiles, such as snakes, that feed on whole animals are less likely to succumb to these problems since they receive a balanced diet. Excessive egg laying can exacerbate a marginal state, giving rise to soft-shelled eggs and egg binding, particularly in lizards. Various combined calcium and Vitamin D_3 supplements are available. You can administer these in the form of a powder on food. To use crickets, either add the vitamin supplement powder to the crickets' food or sprinkle the powder over the crickets just before you feed them to the herptiles. If you feed meat products then use a complete canned cat food; these products are balanced in terms of their vitamin and mineral content. Offal, such as liver, with a very wide calcium to phosphorous ratio in the order of 1:50 will actually precipitate the disorder over a period of time.

Always avoid the excessive use of vitamins, however, particularly in apparently healthy herptiles. Too much Vitamin D_3 can lead to excessive amounts of calcium being liberated into the bloodstream and deposited outside the skeletal system, particularly within the heart and larger arteries. Calcium deposits have also been identified as bladder stones in Green Iguanas.

Using X-rays, a veterinarian can gain an insight into the state of the skeletal system. Green Iguanas kept on a poor diet, for example, show symptoms of calcium deficiency in their hind legs. On radiological examination, the cause of the weakness is all too apparent. If you suspect this condition, be sure to handle the lizard very carefully; its limb bones are liable to break

Below: *An X-ray of the well-calcified skeleton of a Green Iguana after diet correction. Note gravel in gut.*

almost spontaneously – so-called 'greenstick fractures' – in severe cases of this condition.

Parasites
Parasites can be broadly divided into external and internal types. The mites and ticks are the most significant external parasites (ectoparasites) of herptiles. They are rounded creatures related to spiders and adapted to a parasitic way of life.

Ticks Ticks are relatively large parasites (and thus clearly visible to the naked eye) and are often present on newly imported snakes and tortoises. They attach themselves to their hosts by means of piercing mouthparts and swell up as they feed on blood from the tissues. Always remove ticks carefully; if the mouthparts remain embedded in the skin a local infection may develop and spread, giving rise to the condition known as cellulitis. The safest means of persuading a tick to loosen its grip is to smear it in petroleum jelly, which will block its breathing pore. Although not immediate in its effect, this method ensures that the whole tick will soon drop off intact. Life cycles of ticks encountered on reptiles are complex, and may involve intermediate hosts. There is little chance of a population explosion under captive conditions.

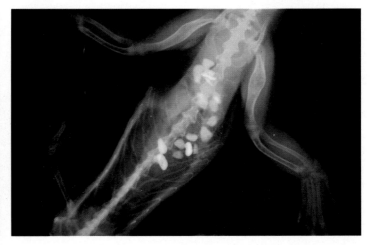

Mites Like ticks, mites feed on the blood of their host, but they are usually present in much greater numbers. They are much less conspicuous than ticks, however, and may be apparent only on close examination. Apart from the risk of causing anaemia and thus death, both these groups of ectoparasites can also spread blood-borne protozoal (unicellular) parasites and other disease organisms.

One of the most widely seen mites is the snake mite (*Ophionyssus natricis*). These are often dark in colour and tend to congregate around the head of the snake. Always treat new stock for mites as a precaution. Keep new snakes in a separate room from established stock, since these ectoparasites are relatively mobile and can spread from cage to cage. Place a matchstick-sized piece of dichlorvos strip (plastic impregnated with the insecticide) in a muslin bag in the vivarium for three or four days. Repeat the treatment weekly to kill off any newly hatched mites. It is well worth taking extra care at this stage, rather than having an epidemic to deal with later on.

In certain instances, evidence suggests that mites may be developing immunity to the traditional dichlorvos treatment. This is most likely to occur on dealers' premises with a large throughput of snakes. If this appears to be the case, then a new group of antiparasitic compounds – the avermectins – can be used. Ivermectin (the most widely used of the avermectins) needs to be given by injection, which is a task for your veterinarian.

Blood parasites Relatively little is known about unicellular (protozoal) parasites in herptiles. Infections of this type are not unknown in tortoises, but the most significant protozoal disease affects snakes. The protozoan concerned, *Entamoeba*, causes severe enteritis in snakes, with blood present in droppings. It is highly contagious and will spread rapidly, although treatment with the specific drug

Above: *The snake mite,* Ophionyssus natricis, *obtained from a Great Plains Rat Snake (magnified × 120).*

metronidazole, obtainable from a veterinarian, can be effective. You must observe strict hygienic precautions, especially to avoid transmitting the infection to other snakes. Other related protozoans that cause similar symptoms may be found in the droppings; they respond to the same treatment.

Intestinal worms A wide variety of intestinal worms, including roundworms and tapeworms, have been reported in reptiles. The effects of infestation vary, from loss of appetite to death. A sample of faecal material can be useful in confirming the presence of such parasites. The life cycles of many of these worms are unrecorded. It is known that they can pass through intermediate hosts, such as fish. Even amphibians can fulfil this role in some cases, with the life cycle of the parasite being completed when the amphibian is eaten by a reptile, such as a snake.

Below: *A tapeworm,* Bothridium pythonis, *taken from the intestine of an African Rock Python.*

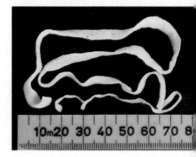

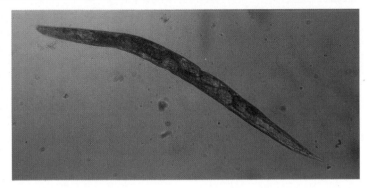

Above: *Amphibians also harbour parasites. This is a female* Rhabdias *roundworm from a White's Tree Frog.*

Roundworms, as their name suggests, are circular in cross-section – rather like an earthworm – and generally whitish in colour. Your veterinarian will prescribe fenbendazole or a similar drug to tackle these worms. Avoid proprietary dog and cat worming preparations; these often contain piperazine which, at an effective dose level, is liable to prove toxic to reptiles. Since dosage is usually calculated on body weight, most veterinarians will allow one third of the total weight for the shell when treating chelonians. It is always worth knowing the weight of your animal when you consult your veterinarian.

Tapeworms, as you would expect, are flat in appearance. You may have to look carefully to spot the characteristic small whitish segments packed with eggs that appear in the droppings of affected animals. Tapeworms are most common in carnivorous species, including snakes and some lizards, and can be treated effectively with tablets or by an injection of praziquantel given by a veterinarian.

Bacterial disease
The relatively slow metabolism of herptiles means that they can be easily overdosed if antibiotics and similar treatments are given regularly. Antibiotics are nevertheless very valuable in combating bacterial disease, providing that medication begins early in the course of the illness. Here we look at a number of bacterial infections that may affect herptiles in captivity.

Septicaemia Septicaemia is a common problem in reptiles. It often causes sudden death with little, if any, prior warning. The bacteria responsible, usually of the Gram-negative group, multiply in the bloodstream. They can be transmitted by mites or ticks, or they may gain access through injuries on the body. One of the characteristic features of septicaemia seen at post-mortem examination is the presence of tiny haemorrhages throughout the body tissues. This may also cause a red discoloration of the skin.

Blood-borne bacterial infections can also lead to the development of localised abscesses. They appear as swellings over the surface of the body, often on the legs in lizards and on the neck in tortoises. These may need surgery to remove the focus of infection.

Respiratory problems These most commonly affect reptiles that have been chilled. A discharge from the nostrils is a typical, but not diagnostic, feature of such infections. Appropriate antibiotic therapy offers the best hope of recovery; your veterinarian will provide a course of injections. Keep affected reptiles at a relatively high temperature and wipe off any discharges so that they do not clog the nostrils.

Above: *It is possible to repair shell damage in chelonians by means of fibreglass, as shown here. The living shell will gradually heal.*

Pneumonia can cause problems in chelonians and demands special treatment from your veterinarian. And aquatic chelonians are not immune from such infections, which usually result from insanitary environmental conditions. Affected individuals swim with difficulty at an abnormal angle in the water and cannot rest in the characteristic horizontal position. Using X-rays to pinpoint the precise location of the infection, a veterinarian may opt to drill a small hole in the shell and administer antibiotics directly to the site of the infection. The shell is basically living tissue and will heal slowly over a period of years. If the shell is severely damaged, the veterinarian can use various resins to hold the parts together while a natural bond develops.

Salmonellosis This is the most significant bacterial infection of reptiles, although in many cases there are few clinical signs. The infection can pass to reptiles in contaminated foodstuffs, such as raw chicken.

The danger lies in the fact that *Salmonella* bacteria harboured by an infected reptile (which may or may not show any signs of disease) could be transmitted to humans, causing the symptoms of food poisoning in most cases. Complications in very young and elderly patients may arise. The risk is real, but the likelihood of human infection is very slight, providing sensible precautions are taken. Always wear gloves when handling terrapins, in particular, and when cleaning out their tank. Unsupervised children are particularly at risk if they are permitted to handle chelonians. Teach them to wash their hands afterwards. Keep equipment from the tank well away from surfaces used for the preparation of food and pour all water down a drain and never down a sink, where bacteria could infect food or plates.

There have been scares over reptile salmonellosis, particularly in the United States, but such precautions should eliminate the risk of the disease being transferred to humans. Indeed, *Salmonella* is a very common environmental contaminant; surveys suggest that it is present on 20 percent of poultry carcasses and 13 percent of coins.

Viral diseases
The viral diseases of herptiles have not been well documented to date. The majority now recognized have been discovered only during the past 15 years or so. Some cause rapid death and as antibiotics prove ineffective there is no treatment in most cases, even if the virus is identified. Some viruses appear specific – affecting iguanas and amievas only, for example – and none can be spread to humans as far as we know.

One of the best recognized viral diseases is viral papilloma of Lacertid lizards. This is transferred by direct contact and, for this reason, males tend to be infected around the head whereas females have the typical warty growths close to the tail. (A male with a head lesion will investigate the tail region of a female before mating, thus passing on the infection. When other males approach the same female the infection spreads.) Viral papillomas can be treated surgically, but often recur at a later stage.

Fungal disease
Aquatic herptiles are most at risk from fungal infections, notably *Trionyx* and Diamond-back

Terrapins, as well as amphibians. (Diamond-back Terrapins usually live in brackish water, however, and this offers some natural protection against infections of this type.) The fungal spores are usually present in the water and often gain access to the body following a superficial injury. The whitish fungal threads over the body surface show up most clearly when the affected animal is immersed in water.

Maintaining clean healthy living conditions for your herptiles is the best way to keep fungal infections at bay. Should fungus develop, transfer the affected animal to a separate container for treatment. The fungus remedies available for tropical fishes can be effective for herptiles. Traditional remedies are based on dyes, such as malachite green and methylene blue. These preparations are absorbed by the filtration system in the tank; during treatment use only the simplest mechanical filter to avoid reducing the efficiency of these remedies. Several modern proprietary treatments are effective against fungus. Your veterinarian can also supply ointments. Since you need to keep the animal out of water for a short time after application, these are more useful for terrapins than for many amphibians.

Below: Viral papillomas on a Green Lizard. These warty growths recurred after surgery, which often happens. They are spread by direct contact.

Life expectancy

The potential lifespan of herptiles can vary considerably, depending on the species concerned. One of the most comprehensive surveys in this field has been undertaken by the Society for the Study of Amphibians and Reptiles, in conjunction with the Philadelphia Herpetological Society. The results suggest that amphibians will live between three and ten years under captive conditions. Among the reptiles, the crocodilians and chelonians have a life expectancy measured in decades, as do some snakes, notably the boids. Some lizards may also live well over ten years, although this would appear to be the exception rather than the rule in most cases.

The shortest lifespan was recorded for chameleons, with no individual in the survey surviving for more than two years. It may be that chameleons have a naturally short lifespan, yet it is not always possible to correlate survival in the wild with that in captivity. Environmental factors can be significant, and the ready availability of food may, in fact, shorten the lifespan of captive herptiles by making them obese. Records from the wild suggest, however, that herptiles generally have a shorter lifespan in their native surroundings. One survey of 66 Zambian Geckos (*Lygodactylus chobiensis*) revealed that none survived for more than 16 months after the study had begun.

Species section

The following section covers a variety of the species that are usually available from pet stores or from herpetological dealers. Those that are likely to be difficult to maintain because of their specialized feeding habits, such as the Egg-eating Snake (*Dasypeltis scabia*), have been omitted, although they can make fascinating vivarium occupants. This particular snake feeds on relatively small eggs, and only the biggest individuals can deal with even young chickens' eggs. In order to keep these snakes, therefore, you will need access to a supply of quails' eggs, for example, on a regular basis. There are commercial breeders of such birds, and if one is nearby it may be possible to obtain infertile eggs, otherwise it can prove very difficult to maintain such snakes successfully. The egg shells, in fact, are regurgitated by the snake, which breaks the egg within its body.

Herptiles that grow too large for the average domestic environ-

ment, or could become a liability because of their size, are also not included here, even if they are occasionally available. A case in point is the Reticulated Python (*Python reticulatus*), which can grow to 10m (33ft) in length and will prove correspondingly difficult to handle, especially in inexperienced hands.

The cost of purchasing herptiles is variable. You can expect to pay a lot less for amphibians, which may also prove easier to feed in captivity than reptiles. It is not always a good idea to choose the largest specimens available; not only will these probably be more costly, but also they will be older and thus may prove more difficult to acclimatize in new surroundings. Keep herptiles of different sizes apart whenever possible, to avoid the risk of bullying and, in some cases, cannibalism. As a general rule, house species on their own unless the surroundings are large and the creatures are known to be completely compatible with each other.

Tortoises, Terrapins and Turtles

Class: REPTILIA – The Reptiles
After ruling the world, the number and diversity of reptiles fell sharply at the end of the Cretaceous Period about 65 million years ago, when countless dinosaurs and similar creatures became extinct. It appears that a change in the world's climate at that time – towards generally colder conditions – was at least partly responsible for the demise of large numbers of species. The reptiles living today are but a pale reflection of the glory of their magnificent ancestors. One in particular, the Tuatara *(Sphenodon punctatus)* from New Zealand, truly represents a 'living fossil' – the only remaining member of the Rhynchocephalia. This burrowing, lizard-like reptile is not available to herpetologists, however. The remaining reptile groups – the tortoises and related forms, the crocodiles, the lizards, and the snakes – are still relatively numerous and mainly restricted to the warmer areas of the world. Since they cannot generate their own body heat, they respond behaviourally to the warmth around them available in the environment.

Chrysemys dorbigni
Slider Terrapin
- **Distribution:** Stretches of the Uruguay River, ranging into the provinces of Corrientes and Entre Rios in Argentina
- **Length:** Up to 25cm (10in)
- **Diet:** Both animal and vegetable matter
- **Ideal conditions:** Water and air temperature in the range of 20-32°C (68-90°F). Plenty of sun. Keep smaller individuals at the higher end of the temperature range
- **Hibernation:** No
- **Sex differences:** Mature males are often darker in colour than females
- **Breeding:** Clutch may consist of between 8 and 17 eggs

Above: **Chrysemys dorbigni**
This colourful species is also known as the Black-bellied Slider, because of its unusually dark plastron (the lower shell surface).

The Slider Terrapins comprising the genus *Chrysemys* occur over a very wide area of the Americas, and although the Red-eared Terrapin is most commonly seen as a pet, other species are occasionally available. This particularly attractive form is a popular pet in Brazil, but is less common (and therefore expensive) in Europe. Its main distinguishing feature is the presence of elongated spots at the corners of the mouth.

Keep these lively terrapins in similar conditions to the Red-eared Slider. (Described on page 64.)

Order: CHELONIA – Tortoises, Terrapins and Turtles
These unmistakable reptiles are characterized by their shells, which serve to encase their bodies. The upper part of the shell is known as the carapace; the lower surface as the plastron. Unfortunately, there is considerable confusion over the common names applied to the chelonians. In the UK, the term 'tortoise' is applied to terrestrial forms, whereas terrapins are regarded as freshwater aquatic species. In UK usage, the name 'turtle' applies exclusively to marine species, which are not described in this book. Yet in the USA and elsewhere, the name 'turtle' is widely used for all chelonians, which frequently leads to confusion. A case in point is the Box Turtle – a common name that applies to two different genera with differing habits. Members of the North American *Terrapene* genus, for example, are much more terrestrial than members of the Asiatic *Cuora* genus. In this section, 'tortoise' refers to essentially land-dwelling chelonians, whereas freshwater species are referred to throughout as 'turtles' or 'terrapins'.

Chrysemys picta
Painted Turtle

- **Distribution:** Southern Canada and Central USA
- **Length:** 15cm (6in)
- **Diet:** Insects, fish and vegetable matter
- **Ideal conditions:** 20-25°C (68-77°F), with adequate light for sunbathing
- **Hibernation:** No
- **Sex differences:** Males have much longer claws on their front feet than females
- **Breeding:** Number of eggs depends upon subspecies concerned

There are four distinctive forms of the Painted Turtle. All are easy to keep, being very similar to the Red-eared Slider in their requirements. They spend considerable periods of time basking on land, but remain constantly alert, not hesitating to scurry into the water if they feel threatened. It is vital, therefore, that you provide easy access both into and out of the water. Also provide a suitable light for basking, if they cannot receive sunlight.

Painted Turtles will lay eggs in captivity, but few people provide the right environment for this to occur. The female of the western race (*Chrysemys picta belli*) may lay as many as 20 eggs in a clutch.

Below:
Chrysemys picta marginata
This is the Midland Painted Turtle, one of four subspecies available.

Chrysemys scripta elegans

Red-eared Slider

- **Distribution:** Eastern USA, southwards into Mexico
- **Length:** Up to 30cm (12in)
- **Diet:** *Tubifex* and other worms, meat, fish, some vegetable matter
- **Ideal conditions:** Water temperature 24-30°C (75-86°F), with a suitable basking area
- **Hibernation:** No
- **Sex differences:** Males are usually smaller and have long front claws
- **Breeding:** Expect up to 12 eggs

Above:
Chrysemys scripta elegans
The small hatchlings usually available should grow quite rapidly, and may need a tank 120cm (48in) long.

The Red-eared Slider is the most universally kept aquatic chelonian. It is farmed commercially in various southern states of America and large numbers of hatchlings are exported every year. Breeding farms have also been set up in other countries, including Malaysia. Red-eared Sliders ('slider' refers to their habit of scurrying into water when frightened) are characterised by the red stripes behind their eyes. Young specimens are particularly delightful, but their beautifully marked green shells turn much darker as they mature.

You must keep Red-eared Sliders warm to encourage them to eat. At first, you may need to offer them live food such as *Tubifex* or small earthworms. Gradually, they will learn to accept inanimate foodstuffs and may feed from the hand.

Occasionally, you may come across a number of other related subspecies, notably the Yellow-belly Slider (*Chrysemys scripta scripta*). In this case the markings behind the eyes are yellowish rather than red. Care is identical to that outlined above.

Cuora species
Asiatic Box Turtles
- **Distribution:** Southeast Asia
- **Length:** About 17.5cm (7in)
- **Diet:** *Tubifex* and other worms, meat, fish, some vegetable matter
- **Ideal conditions:** Water and air temperature in the range 24-30°C (75-86°F)
- **Hibernation:** No
- **Sex differences:** A male displays by stretching his head towards the female and biting at her hind limbs
- **Breeding:** Small clutches, perhaps only two eggs

Asiatic Box Turtles are mainly aquatic, although they will spend periods of time on land. The name 'Box Turtle' comes from the hinges on the plastron that enable these chelonians to seal the whole body within the shell, forming a box when danger threatens. Tame individuals are less likely to react in this way when handled, but some always remain nervous.

You are quite likely to obtain the Amboina or Malayan species (*C.amboinensis*), which is characterized by bright yellow bands on the head, but related forms are comparatively rare. Some, such as *C.galbinifrons*, may actually feed on land.

Below: **Cuora amboinensis**
This turtle can prove a shy species.

Geochelone carbonaria
Red-footed Tortoise
- **Distribution:** Much of tropical South America
- **Length:** Up to 44cm (17.3in)
- **Diet:** Varied, with some animal matter, but they often show a preference for fruit, particularly plums
- **Ideal conditions:** An extensive indoor heated enclosure with adequate retreats and a temperature in excess of 25°C (77°F)
- **Hibernation:** No
- **Sex differences:** Males have a concave plastron
- **Breeding:** Up to 15 eggs may be laid

The overall coloration of these chelonians is quite variable; paler individuals are easily confused with the closely-related Yellow-footed Tortoise (*G.denticulata*). It is possible to distinguish between them on the basis of differences in the shell structure. In addition, the lower surface (the plastron) tends to be largely unpigmented in the case of the Red-footed Tortoise.

Red-footed Tortoises are essentially forest dwellers and dislike bright light. Always provide suitable retreats in their enclosure to make them feel at home. Repeated breedings in captivity have been recorded; the female raises herself when she is ready to mate. The nesting chamber may be 23cm (9in) deep to accommodate the eggs.

Left: **Geochelone carbonaria**
These tortoises vary quite widely in their markings, with young hatchlings often being most colourful, as here.

Geochelone elongata
Yellow Tortoise
● **Distribution:** Southeast Asia
● **Length:** Up to 28cm (11in)
● **Diet:** Shows a preference for fruit
● **Ideal conditions:** Secluded environment at about 25°C (77°F)
● **Hibernation:** No
● **Sex differences:** Males have slightly concave plastrons
● **Breeding:** About four eggs per clutch

This species is also known as the Elongated Tortoise because of its relatively long, narrow shape. These tortoises can prove rather shy,

particularly when first obtained. They are often more active at dawn and dusk, rather than during the day. At the onset of the breeding season, the yellowish head takes on a pinkish tinge. This is reflected in the native name 'Laik nakhonga' which means 'red-nosed tortoise'. Another similar species from Southeast Asia is the Travancore Tortoise (*G. travancoria*), although this is rarely available as a pet.

Below: **Geochelone elongata**
Although usually known as the Yellow Tortoise, some of these tortoises can have heavily pigmented carapaces.

Geochelone pardalis
Leopard Tortoise
● **Distribution:** Much of Africa, from Sudan and Ethiopa to Cape province
● **Length:** Up to 45cm (18in)
● **Diet:** Prefers greenstuff to fruit, and rarely takes animal matter
● **Ideal conditions:** Large heated enclosure at around 25°C (77°F)
● **Hibernation:** No
● **Sex differences:** Males have slightly concave plastrons
● **Breeding:** Reputed to lay up to 30 eggs in a clutch, although captive clutches are invariably smaller

Young Leopard Tortoises are basically cream in colour with attractive brown markings on their shells. Unfortunately, the shell

patterning dulls over in older individuals. Keep the youngsters warm and out of draughts. They have voracious appetites and can grow to a considerable size. When they are adult you can allow them to roam freely outdoors on sunny days during the summer.

The females mature when they reach a length of about 38cm (15in) and breeding success has been recorded from around the world. As in many reptiles, the hatching period has proved quite variable, ranging from 111 to 246 days. This wide variation reflects the incubation temperature of the eggs.

Right: **Geochelone pardalis**
The markings of this species are also quite variable, reflecting its wide distribution over much of Africa.

Graptemys geographica
Map Turtle

- **Distribution:** From the Great Lakes to Wisconsin; the Mississippi region from Minnesota southwards to Alabama and Arkansas; New York southwards to Maryland
- **Length:** Up to 23cm (9in)
- **Diet:** Worms, fish, meat, vegetable matter
- **Ideal conditions:** 20-25°C (68-77°F). Keep hatchlings at the warmer end of this temperature range
- **Hibernation:** No
- **Sex differences:** Females grow about twice as large as males
- **Breeding:** Clutches of up to 13 eggs have been recorded

The various Map Turtles are named after their unusual markings, said to

Above: **Graptemys geographica**
Young Map Turtles are much more colourful than their older relatives.

resemble the markings on a map. They are also sometimes known as Sawbacks because of the raised, serrated pattern of the vertebral shields.

The males mature much more rapidly than females, which continue to grow at a slower rate and reach a much greater size. These are not difficult turtles to maintain. They often show a preference for snails, which form a significant part of their diet in the wild. In this particular species, the head is relatively slim, but in related species from the coastal regions of the Gulf of Mexico the head is enlarged to enable them to cope with the hard-shelled molluscs on which they feed.

Kinixys belliana
Bell's Hingeback Tortoise
- **Distribution:** Much of Africa, from Senegal south to Natal
- **Length:** 20cm (8in)
- **Diet:** Vegetable matter, fruit, some meat, mealworms
- **Ideal conditions:** Temperature about 25°C (77°F). Provide a shallow dish of water for bathing
- **Hibernation:** No
- **Sex differences:** Males have much longer tails than females
- **Breeding:** Expect clutches of about four eggs

Bell's is one of the three species of Hingeback Tortoise that range over much of Africa. The common name stems from the hinge at the back of the plastron, which protects them from attack. They have a fairly upright gait, rather like the Red-footed Tortoise.

Hingebacks dislike bright sunlight and do best in subdued lighting. They will aestivate (i.e. go into a dormant state) in the wild under dry conditions; if you find it difficult to persuade a newly-acquired individual to eat, provide a shallow bath of warm water. It may respond by drinking a surprising amount of fluid. Of the related species, the Eroded Kinixys (*K. erosa*) can be recognized by its flared marginal shields; Home's Hingeback (*K. homeana*) is similar to Bell's, but possesses a nuchal scute (at the front of the carapace) in most cases.

Below: **Kinixys belliana**
Bell's Hingeback Tortoise, showing the curved rear of the carapace.

Kinosternon subrubrum
Common Mud Turtle
- **Distribution:** Eastern half of the USA
- **Length:** 10cm (4in)
- **Diet:** *Tubifex* and other worms, meat, fish, vegetable matter
- **Ideal conditions:** Temperature in the range 20-25°C (68-77°F), with basking facilities
- **Hibernation:** No
- **Sex differences:** The male has a relatively concave plastron
- **Breeding:** A typical clutch contains three of four eggs

These turtles are fairly dull in coloration, and remain small. They are easy to cater for, however, although at first they may attempt to bite when handled and are capable of inflicting a painful wound. They also secrete a highly unpleasant odour if they feel threatened. They are unlikely to become mature before four years of age; their small size makes them an ideal species to breed in the home.

Right: **Kinosternon subrubrum**
Ideal for an aquatic vivarium.

Macrochelys temmincki

Alligator Snapping Turtle

- **Distribution:** Southeast USA
- **Length:** In excess of 60cm (24in)
- **Diet:** Worms, meat, fish, some vegetable matter
- **Ideal conditions:** Suitably large accommodation
- **Hibernation:** No
- **Sex differences:** The vent of the male is positioned further from the shell than in females
- **Breeding:** Expect up to 50 eggs in a clutch

These sedentary giants may appear very attractive when newly emerged from the egg, but they are likely to outgrow their accommodation rapidly. In the wild these 'snappers', as they are popularly known in the USA, remain motionless on the river bed with their mouths open to catch passing fish. On the floor of the mouth there is a pinkish filament resembling a worm. This can be moved independently of the head and thus acts as a tempting lure. Fishes that attempt to eat the 'worm' are quickly snapped up and swallowed by the turtle.

Alligator Snapping Turtles are thought to mature when over ten years old, at a shell length of about 35cm (14in). The Common Snapping Turtle (*Chelydra serpentina*) is very similar and equally sluggish in behaviour.

Below: **Macrochelys temmincki**
One of the giants among freshwater chelonians. The Common Snapper is somewhat smaller, but requires similarly spacious accommodation.

Malaclemys terrapin
Diamond-back Terrapin
- **Distribution:** Salty marshland along the eastern seaboard of the USA
- **Length:** Up to 23cm (9in)
- **Diet:** Worms, fish, meat
- **Ideal conditions:** Temperature 20-25°C (68-77°F). Dissolve a small amount of salt in their water to minimise the risk of fungus
- **Hibernation:** No
- **Sex differences:** Males are invariably smaller than females, with narrower heads
- **Breeding:** Up to 12 eggs are likely

The Diamond-back is known as a terrapin because of its preference for brackish water. (The early settlers of North America coined the term 'terrapin' for species that lived in neither salty nor fresh water). It was once considered to be endangered because of its popularity among gourmets.

Seven distinct races are recognized on the grounds of differences in coloration. All are powerful swimmers. They also leave the water to bask, and so be sure to provide a suitable dry area in their accommodation.

Below: **Malaclemys terrapin**
The Diamond-back varies considerably in its coloration. It used to be famed for its meat, causing wild populations to become scarce.

Terrapene carolina
Common Box Tortoise
- **Distribution:** Eastern side of the USA
- **Length:** In the range 10-12.5cm (4-5in)
- **Diet:** Essentially carnivorous, but may take some vegetable matter
- **Ideal conditions:** Relatively shaded environment, with accessible water
- **Hibernation:** For a short period, if in good health
- **Sex differences:** Males invariably have red rather than brown eyes
- **Breeding:** Up to seven eggs can form a clutch

An increasing number of these tortoises have become available in Europe during recent years, as the Mediterranean *Testudo* species are no longer obtainable. Box Tortoises differ significantly in their habits, however, seeking invertebrates such as snails and earthworms in relatively damp surroundings. Be sure to provide a broad shallow water container in which they can immerse themselves.

Individuals vary quite widely in their markings; some are much more striking than others, both in terms of their shell and body coloration. In common with the *Cuora* turtles, these tortoises have a hinged plastron and are capable of withdrawing their bodies totally within the shell.

Right: **Terrapene carolina**
Box Tortoises rank among the longest lived reptiles; some are said to have lived for over a century. They can be sexed by eye colour.

Mauremys caspica
Caspian Turtle

- **Distribution:** Northern and eastern Mediterranean, extending to Iran
- **Length:** 20cm (8in)
- **Diet:** *Tubifex* and other worms, meat, fish, some vegetable matter
- **Ideal conditions:** Water temperature 24-30°C (75-86°F), with a suitable basking area
- **Hibernation:** No
- **Sex differences:** Males have their genito-anal openings further from the base of the tail than females
- **Breeding:** Expect up to eight eggs in a clutch

In the wild, these relatively dull turtles often live in stagnant stretches of water, sometimes having heavy infestations of algae on their shells. In severe cases,

Above: **Mauremys caspica**
Large numbers of Caspian Turtles may congregate in areas of water through their range, which includes arid areas of the Arabian Gulf.

these algal patches spread under the shields, raising them up to give the shell an uneven appearance.

Caspian Turtles are among the hardiest of aquatic chelonians. You can keep adults outdoors in a pond during the warmer months of the year; care for the hatchlings indoors, however, where you can keep a check on their appetites. In order to avoid polluting the water of the pond with real meat foods, you can usually persuade these turtles to take pond pellets produced for fishes; these are perfectly suitable as a diet. Never include fishes in the pond with turtles, however, since the turtles are likely to attack and perhaps eat the fishes.

Testudo graeca
*Mediterranean Spur-thighed
Tortoise*

- **Distribution:** In the countries bordering the Mediterranean Sea
- **Length:** Up to about 30cm (12in), females generally bigger
- **Diet:** Primarily vegetarian, but will also take some animal matter
- **Ideal conditions:** Outside enclosure for sunny days; inside accommodation at 20°C (68°F) upwards
- **Hibernation:** Yes, in the case of large individuals of suitable weight
- **Sex differences:** Males have concave plastrons
- **Breeding:** Usually four eggs. In some cases, up to 13 eggs can form the clutch

The commercial trade in these tortoises was banned under a European Community order during 1983, allegedly because it was endangering wild populations. Yet CITES regard this species as being suitable for controlled trade (see page 16). In the past, large numbers were exported and kept under unsuitable conditions, which led to their premature demise. Properly cared for, however, these tortoises will breed regularly and live for decades in captivity. Their sale and movement is now only permitted under licence in some countries, including the UK. This also applies to captive-bred individuals. Such regulations do nothing to encourage large-scale breeding of these chelonians, since surplus stock is difficult to sell as a result.

The characteristic feature of this active species is the presence of tubercles in the vicinity of the thighs.

Above: **Testudo graeca**
The two spurs occur on the thighs, one on either side of the tail.

Testudo hermanni

Hermann's Tortoise

- **Distribution:** Northern Mediterranean region, confined to Europe
- **Length:** 18cm (7in)
- **Diet:** Both plant and animal matter. Said to be more omnivorous than the preceding species
- **Ideal conditions:** Outside enclosure and inside accommodation, both providing a temperature of 20°C (68°F) upwards
- **Hibernation:** Yes, in the case of large individuals of suitable weight
- **Sex differences:** Males have much longer tails than females
- **Breeding:** Average clutch contains three eggs

Although superficially similar to the Mediterranean Spur-thighed Tortoise, this species has no spurs and the tail tapers to a point rather than having a rounded appearance. Young tortoises appear to be mature by their seventh year. At this age, the females produce smaller eggs than those of older females, which also applies in other species. The eggs normally hatch about eight weeks after laying. There is no fixed time, however, and it may vary by a month or more in some cases.

These tortoises were also exported from their natural habitat along with the Mediterranean Spur-thighed Tortoise and are now subject to the same prohibitive regulations on commercial trade.

Left: **Testudo hermanni**
The sexes of this species are of similar size; in the Mediterranean Spur-thighed, males are invariably smaller than their prospective mates.

Trionyx ferox

Florida Softshell Turtle

- **Distribution:** Florida, extending into southern Georgia and South Carolina, USA
- **Length:** Up to 50cm (20in)
- **Diet:** Worms, meat and fish
- **Ideal conditions:** Predominantly aquatic environment with shallow water and a muddy base for burrowing.
- **Hibernation:** No
- **Sex differences:** Females grow significantly larger than males
- **Breeding:** May lay up to 22 eggs

This representative of the genus is the largest of the North American species. The shell is soft and leathery. These shy turtles spend much of their time in shallow water, superbly camouflaged on the bottom, using their elongated nostrils to breathe at the water's surface. They can be very aggressive when housed together, so take care to ensure that all have an equal opportunity to feed.

An American form known as the Spiny Softshell (*T.spinifer*) is often available; the name comes from the spiny projections around the edge of the carapace. Other species from different regions of the world are also occasionally available.

Right: **Trionyx ferox**
This is one of the largest of the soft-shelled turtles. Other related forms are found in Asia and Africa.

Crocodiles, Caimans, Alligators

The crocodilians are one of the oldest surviving groups of reptiles, having changed little from the age of the dinosaurs over 100 million years ago. Various regulations in different countries govern the keeping of these reptiles as 'pets'. Hatchlings, if cared for properly, will grow quickly and soon need larger accommodation. Their sharp teeth and powerful tails make them a liability in the home, particularly as many species can grow over 4.5m (15ft).

Below: **Caiman crocodilus**
Spectacled Caimans, in common with other crocodilians, must have access to an area of dry land where they can bask beneath a heat lamp. In suitable conditions, they live for decades.

Caiman crocodilus
Spectacled Caiman

- **Distribution:** Tropical South America
- **Length:** Up to 2.4m (8ft)
- **Diet:** Carnivorous. Offer whole items, such as pinkies, older mice and day-old chicks, depending on the caiman's size
- **Ideal conditions:** Warm surroundings with a minimum temperature of 25°C (77°F). Provide a suitable basking area beneath a heat source
- **Hibernation:** No
- **Sex differences:** Males have a distinctive roar. (Unlike other reptiles, crocodilians are surprisingly vocal.)
- **Breeding:** Not in domestic surroundings

These caimans are often imported as hatchlings to the USA for the pet trade; many more are killed for their skins. They are surprisingly susceptible to low temperatures. Other species, such as the Dwarf Caiman (*Paleosuchus palpebrosus*), may grow to a length of only 1.2m (4ft) and are thus preferable to the larger species. They still need careful handling, however, and suitably spacious accommodation to thrive.

Lizards

Order: SQUAMATA/Suborder: LACERTALIA – Lizards

With over 3,000 species recognized, there is considerable diversity in the appearance of lizards. Two American lizards, the Gila Monster (*Heloderma suspectum*) and the Beaded Lizard (*H.horridum*) are poisonous. The most unusual members of this group are undoubtedly the Amphisbaenians, the so-called 'Worm Lizards'. As their common name suggests, these lizards are similar to worms in appearance. They can grow up to 1m (39in) in length and live entirely underground, feeding mostly on invertebrates. They are rarely available to herpetologists. Some authorities claim they are not true lizards but should be classified in a group of their own.

The lizards commonly available as 'pets' are more 'conventional' in appearance. The major Families include the agamids (found exclusively in Eurasia, Africa and Australasia), the iguanids (confined to the Americas) and the extraordinary chameleons from Africa, India and Madagascar.

Agama agama
Common Agama

- **Distribution:** Central Africa
- **Length:** 30cm (12in)
- **Diet:** Mainly insects, but may take some fruit
- **Ideal conditions:** Spacious surroundings, with retreats and basking facilities. Temperature up to 30°C (86°F)
- **Hibernation:** No
- **Sex differences:** Dominant males have red heads
- **Breeding:** Clutches may contain 12 eggs

If you keep a group of these lizards, be prepared for fighting to occur if

Above: **Agama agama**
A male Common Agama, as shown by its characteristic bright red head.

there is more than one male in the vivarium. They are often highly territorial; a male has a group of several females, which he defends determinedly from potential rivals. Mating is preceded by a head-bobbing display; the resulting eggs may take seven weeks or so to hatch. Offer the young agamas small insects as their first food.

Agamas are similar to the iguanids of the Americas, although the two groups are quite distinct in their geographical distribution.

Ameiva ameiva
Ameiva

- **Distribution:** Central and South America
- **Length:** 50cm (20in)
- **Diet:** Mainly insects and small animals, but will take some vegetable matter
- **Ideal conditions:** Temperature 28-30°C (82-86F), with suitable retreats
- **Hibernation:** No
- **Sex differences:** Females are smaller, with smaller jaws and greener overall coloration than males
- **Breeding:** Clutch size varies between two and eight eggs

These active and often territorial lizards need relatively spacious surroundings to thrive in captivity. Ameivas respond well to black lights (ultraviolet fluorescent tubes) above the vivarium to provide the beneficial UV wavelengths of sunlight.

They have been bred successfully under vivarium conditions and, although display can be protracted, mating itself is very rapid. The female will swell with eggs, and before laying she will excavate a shallow depression in the vivarium substrate. The nest site is capped with a dome of excavated material. Unfortunately, Ameivas will often eat their own eggs, so remove the eggs from the vivarium and incubate them artificially.

Related lizards are described as Racerunners or Whiptails, and need similar care to the Ameiva.

Below: **Ameiva ameiva**
Twenty species of these lively but nervous lizards are known. They are also described as Jungle Runners.

Anguis fragilis
Slow Worm
- **Distribution:** Europe, extending into Asia and North Africa
- **Length:** 30cm (12in) on average
- **Diet:** Insects, but they will also take garden slugs
- **Ideal conditions:** Vivarium temperature of 15-22°C (59-72°F), with suitable retreats
- **Hibernation:** Yes
- **Sex differences:** Males are greyish brown; females tend to be more coppery, with a black line running down the back
- **Breeding:** Up to 15 live young

Slow Worms appear more closely related to snakes than lizards, since they lack external limbs. Nevertheless, their internal anatomy shows traces of a walking mode of locomotion, and they have eyelids, which are also characteristic of lizards.

You can keep Slow Worms out of doors in a suitable vivarium during the summer in temperate climates. They spend much of their time buried and are relatively inactive. Perhaps such inactivity accounts for their long lifespan; one individual kept at Copenhagen Museum lived for over half a century, and others have lived in excess of 30 years.

A similar, but much larger, lizard is the European Glass Lizard (*Ophisaurus apodus*). It can grow to a length of 120cm (48in)

Below: **Anguis fragilis**
Slow Worms are long-lived lizards.

Anolis carolinensis
Green Anole
- **Distribution:** Southeastern United States
- **Length:** 18cm (7in)
- **Diet:** Insects and fruit
- **Ideal conditions:** 23-29°C (73-84°F)
- **Hibernation:** No
- **Sex differences:** Males are bigger and more colourful than females
- **Breeding:** Relatively small clutches, possibly only two eggs

A member of the Family Iguanidae, this particular species is frequently available and thus very well known to herpetologists. In common with other anoles, the Green Anole can change its colour quite dramatically depending on the temperature and the surroundings. This ability has earned anoles the name of 'American chameleons'. Anoles also share with true chameleons the habit of drinking from drops of vegetation. If you keep anoles, you may find it more effective to spray the vivarium rather than provide a water bowl.

Males engage in elaborate display rituals and may be aggressive to one another; always house them separately, out of sight of each other. Green Anoles will breed in captivity, although the eggs do not always hatch well. They may be buried or hidden beneath vegetation. These lizards can often become quite tame.

Right: **Anolis carolinensis**
Able to inflate skin under the throat.

Basilicus species
Basilisk

- **Distribution:** Tropical America
- **Length:** Up to 60cm (24in)
- **Diet:** Small animals and fruit
- **Ideal conditions:** Spacious surroundings with water. Temperature 23-30°C (73-86°F)
- **Hibernation:** No
- **Sex differences:** Females are smaller than males and lack the crest (as do juveniles of both sexes)
- **Breeding:** Up to 20 eggs may be laid

Basilisks are active lizards that typically live near water. Not only do they swim well, but their slender toes also enable them to run over the surface of the water to escape predators. You will need to provide a fairly spacious vivarium for these lizards if they are to display their natural beauty and agility.

There are five species of basilisks, which can be distinguished on the basis of their head ornamentation. A similar group of lizards known as Water Dragons (*Hydrosaurus* species) have evolved in Southeast Asia, although these are related to the agamids rather than iguanids.

Below: **Basilicus plumifrons**
Plumed or Double-crested Basilisk.

Chamaeleo jacksoni

Jackson's Chameleon
- **Distribution:** East Africa
- **Length:** Up to 40cm (16in)
- **Diet:** Varied, must include winged live food
- **Ideal conditions:** Temperature is less critical than in other lizards, but be sure to provide adequate space
- **Hibernation:** No
- **Sex differences:** Males are thinner overall than females
- **Breeding:** Females give birth to as many as 30 live young

The fascinating habits of these essentially tree-living lizards are well known; the ability to change colour, the unusual rotating eyes, the long tongues and specialized digits make chameleons unmistakable. Unfortunately, they are among the most shortlived of lizards, rarely living for more than one year. Some

Above: **Chamaeleo jacksoni**
Males alone possess the three horns.

species produce eggs; others give birth to live young.

In captivity, most chameleons refuse to drink from a bowl, and so you will need to spray part of the vivarium and provide good ventilation. You can allow chameleons to roam free in a greenhouse where the temperature will not fall below about 20°C (68°F). Ensure that they have access to a variety of suitable prey under these conditions. Jackson's Chameleon can cope with adult crickets. Do not keep these chameleons with smaller lizards; they may eat them.

This species has been bred successfully under vivarium conditions, usually producing litters in the autumn. Be sure to provide suitable small live food for rearing purposes, e.g. hatchling crickets.

Eublepharis macularius

Leopard Gecko
- **Distribution:** Western Asia
- **Length:** Up to 25cm (10in)
- **Diet:** Insects
- **Ideal conditions:** Temperature in the range 23-30°C (73-86°F)
- **Hibernation:** No, but provide a slightly lower temperature during the winter
- **Sex differences:** Males are bigger than females overall, with pre-anal pores
- **Breeding:** Clutches consist of two eggs

Leopard Geckos have proved among the easiest of this particular group of lizards to breed in the vivarium. As with other geckos, male Leopard Geckos may fight among themselves; always house them on their own or with several females. Eggs are laid during the second year of life, the female burying them in the substrate. They can take up to 14 weeks to hatch, although nine weeks is more usual in warm surroundings. Young Leopard Geckos are banded in appearance and more brightly coloured than the adults.

Below: **Eublepharis macularius**
Leopard Geckos are typically most active at dusk. Easy to breed.

Eumeces fasciatus

Five-lined Skink
- **Distribution:** North America
- **Length:** 15cm (6in)
- **Diet:** Mainly insects
- **Ideal conditions:** Temperature in the range 20-30°C (68-86°F)
- **Hibernation:** No
- **Sex differences:** Males have orange heads
- **Breeding:** Up to 12 eggs may be laid in the substrate

Some confusion exists over the common name of this species, since another skink (*Mabuya quinquetaeniata*) is also known as the Five-lined Skink. The species described here is typical of the group, however, with its flattish appearance and rather secretive habits. The colourful blue tails of young skinks serve to confuse predators, and are readily shed if handled. (This is a fairly common natural 'escape mechanism' among lizards, see page 17.) Provide fairly secluded surroundings in the vivarium for these skinks. In certain species, females remain close to the eggs and may even incubate them in some instances.

Right: **Eumeces fasciatus**
A young Five-lined Skink, as revealed by its blue (and readily shed) tail.

Gekko gecko
Tokay Gecko
- **Distribution:** Asia
- **Length:** 35cm (14in)
- **Diet:** Insects; larger individuals may take pinkies
- **Ideal conditions:** Temperature in the range 23-32°C (73-90°F)
- **Hibernation:** No
- **Sex differences:** Males have pre-anal pores
- **Breeding:** Pairs of eggs that may take three to six months to hatch

These geckos are attractively coloured but they can be aggressive; large individuals have a powerful bite. They are quite able to take adult crickets, and some will even consume small mice if given an opportunity. Breeding females may lay their eggs on the sides of the vivarium; they will stick to the walls. It is difficult to move them without damaging them. The safest thing to do is to cover the eggs with a ventilated plastic container and remove the young geckos when they hatch. If you provide a length of hollow plastic tubing of the appropriate diameter, the lizards will often lay their eggs inside. You can then transfer the tube complete with the eggs to separate accommodation for hatching.

Left: **Gekko gecko**
Tokay Geckos, showing the slit-like pupils of the eye typical of nocturnal members of the Gekkonidae.

83

Iguana iguana
Green Iguana
- **Distribution:** Central and South America
- **Length:** Up to 150cm (60in)
- **Diet:** Plant matter and insects
- **Ideal conditions:** In the range 26-35°C (79-95°F), with suitable basking facilities
- **Hibernation:** No
- **Sex differences:** Males have more developed skin flaps on the head than females
- **Breeding:** A clutch may consist of 40 eggs

The Green Iguana is commonly available and easy to maintain, although as adults they need plenty of space. They may well bathe if you provide a suitable area of water for them. Males tend to be highly territorial. They maintain a number of females and fight off any potential rivals. The body coloration can vary quite widely, which is a reflection of their extensive distribution. Some individuals are a particularly striking shade of emerald green.

Below: **Iguana iguana**
Green Iguanas can grow quite large.

Lacerta viridis
Green Lizard
- **Distribution:** The Mediterranean region
- **Length:** Up to 40cm (16in)
- **Diet:** Mainly insects
- **Ideal conditions:** Provide a range of temperatures in the vivarium, plus adequate retreats
- **Hibernation:** No
- **Sex differences:** Males are often brighter than females, with bigger heads and obvious femoral pores
- **Breeding:** Clutches consist of anything from 6 to 20 eggs

The Lacertid lizards (not found in the Americas) reach their greatest diversity in the Mediterranean region, where a vast number of forms have evolved on the various islands. All share the facility to shed the tail as an escape mechanism when attacked by a predator. The anatomy of the tail region is adapted for this purpose, so that minimum damage is caused to the lizard. Once detached, the tail gyrates on the ground for a few minutes as an additional means of diverting a potential predator. Needless to say, you should handle these lizards very carefully. Limited regeneration of the tail stump is possible.

The Green Lizard is ideal for keeping in captivity. You can house it in an outdoor vivarium during the warm months of the year. Take particular care during the breeding season, however, to prevent any individuals being persecuted by dominant members of a group. Even females can disagree at this time; you may need to separate them to prevent fatalities.

Right: **Lacerta viridis**
Sometimes called the Emerald Lizard, because of its bright green colour. An ideal 'pet' species.

Phelsuma cepediana
Day Gecko

● **Distribution:** Mauritius
● **Length:** 10-15cm (4-6in)
● **Diet:** Insects; will also feed on a honey solution
● **Ideal conditions:** Temperature in the range 25-30°C (77-86°F). Provide adequate cover and space for climbing
● **Hibernation:** No
● **Sex differences:** Males have pronounced femoral pores
● **Breeding:** Two eggs form the usual clutch

This gecko is one of 28 species that live on islands in the Indian Ocean. They range in size from about 10cm(4in) to the 25cm(10in) Madagascar species. The markings can prove variable, even between individuals of the same species, and the bright green coloration can darken in individuals that are harassed or sick. These geckos feed on nectar in the wild and will accept a honey solution in the vivarium. Their pupils are round rather than slit-like as in other geckos, indicating that they are active during the hours of daylight. They are highly territorial; be sure to

Above: **Phelsuma cepediana**
Day Geckos are colourful and lively vivarium occupants, often becoming quite tame under captive conditions.

house pairs alone as the males will invariably fight within the confines of the vivarium.

Day Geckos can prove prolific breeders, producing as many as 24 clutches of eggs in a year. It is advisable to provide a calcium supplement, such as powdered cuttlefish, to prevent egg binding.

Podarcis muralis
Wall Lizard

- **Distribution:** Europe, extending to Western Asia
- **Length:** 20cm (8in)
- **Diet:** Mainly insects
- **Ideal conditions:** Vivarium temperature 23-26°C (73-79°F)
- **Hibernation:** No
- **Sex differences:** Males are invariably brighter in coloration than females
- **Breeding:** Between three and eight eggs in a typical clutch

Above: **Podarcis muralis**
Wall Lizards are often seen basking in the wild on rocks, trees or walls.

Fourteen subspecies of this particular Wall Lizard are recognized, and some variation in coloration between individuals is quite normal. They are often found in areas where grapes are grown, but the use of potent insecticides has severely affected their distribution. In a vivarium keep them in groups, headed by a male.

Other species of Wall Lizard are often kept under vivarium conditions, such as the Ruin Lizard found in Italy and also in parts of Yugoslavia. Occasionally, predominantly black individuals are seen; these are termed as melanistic.

Varanus niloticus
Nile Monitor

- **Distribution:** Africa
- **Length:** 2m (6.5ft)
- **Diet:** Insects when young, meat when mature
- **Ideal conditions:** A very large area is required, with a powerful heat lamp for basking that gives a localized temperature as high as 35°C (95°F)
- **Hibernation:** No
- **Sex differences:** Males have broader heads than females
- **Breeding:** Clutches of 30 eggs may be laid. Hatching occurs after three months

Although monitors have a wide distribution – extending from Africa into Australasia – it is the African species that are most commonly kept. The Nile Monitor is typical of the genus. It is colourful when young and grows rapidly when kept under suitable conditions. Monitors are extremely active lizards; you will need to provide adequate space, both for climbing and swimming, as well as a basking area. They often eat eggs and will readily accept them as part of their diet in captive surroundings.

The other African species frequently available is Bosc's Monitor (*V.exanthematicus*), which is rather duller in colour than the Nile Monitor. The same applies to the Asiatic Water Monitor (*V.salvator*), which, as its name suggests, must have access to a reasonable area of water to feel completely 'at home'.

Below: **Varanus niloticus**
Young Nile Monitors like this one are highly attractive, but they become duller in coloration and more difficult to manage as they mature.

Snakes

Order: SQUAMATA/Suborder: SERPENTES – Snakes
Within the elongated bodies of snakes, the internal organs have undergone some modification. The left lung is invariably smaller than the right, for example, and may even be absent in some cases. The stomach is also elongated, as is the liver and the other body organs. Unlike limbless lizards, snakes lack external ears and ear drums and consequently cannot hear sounds in the accepted sense. They respond to low-frequency vibrations, however, but rarely use this method to pinpoint prey; such vibrations usually herald the approach of danger and send the snake scuttling for safety. Although snakes respond well to movement, their eyesight is not as acute as

Boa constrictor

Boa Constrictor
● **Distribution:** Central and South America
● **Length:** Up to 4m (13ft)
● **Diet:** Rodents, chickens and rabbits
● **Ideal conditions:** Minimum temperature around 24°C (75°F), rising to 30°C (86°F)
● **Hibernation:** No
● **Sex differences:** Males have bigger spurs than females
● **Breeding:** 20-60 live young can be anticipated

These snakes are popular vivarium occupants, and invariably thrive, providing they are not exposed to low temperatures. In the wild, Boa Constrictors spend much of their time in trees and similar vegetation and thus need a relatively tall vivarium with plenty of climbing space. Most Boa Constrictors in good health will take dead food without difficulty.

Healthy Boas will usually start to breed once they reach about 1.5m (5ft) in length, although success may vary from year to year. Before mating, the male uses his spurs (located on either side of the cloaca) to stimulate the female. The spurs are remnants of the hind limbs and are also present in pythons as well as boas. Live young are born about six months after mating and are able to take mice without difficulty, even at this early stage of their lives.

Boa Constrictors are long-lived snakes; records suggest that they may live for more than 40 years.

Below: **Boa constrictor**
Young individuals settle well under vivarium surroundings. They can double their length in the first year.

it appears from their hypnotic stare. By far the most well-developed senses that snakes use to locate potential prey are a combination of taste and smell and, in some snakes, a keen sensitivity to heat. The constantly flicking tongue transfers scent particles to a pair of highly sensitive cavities in the roof of the mouth that make up the Jacobsen's organ. Many snakes use the sensitivity of this organ to follow the scent trails of their prey. Snakes also possess a fine sense of smell. Some snakes are also equipped with a pair of heat sensors between the eyes and nostrils that enable them to detect warm-blooded prey in total darkness. All snakes feed on animals and use various combinations of these senses in their hunt for food.

Drymarchon corais
Indigo Snake
- **Distribution:** From the southeastern United States as far south as Argentina
- **Length:** Up to about 2.7m (9ft)
- **Diet:** Mammals, fish, birds and eggs
- **Ideal conditions:** Large area, temperature 25-30°C (77-86°F)
- **Hibernation:** Temperature 15-20°C (59-68°F) in winter
- **Sex differences:** Tail shape
- **Breeding:** Up to 12 eggs are produced

Above: **Drymarchon corais**
Indigo snakes vary widely in their coloration. This darker race is from the southeastern United States.

This snake is also sometimes known as the Gopher Snake because it is found in the burrows of the Gopher Tortoise (*Gopherus* species). Coloration depends on the area of origin; the Florida race (*D.c.coupei*) is considered the most desirable, being glossy black overall, sometimes with red markings close to the mouth. Specimens from further south in the range are predominantly brownish and much less striking. Although it may hiss when threatened, the Florida race is also less aggressive than the southerly Indigo Snakes, which can be difficult to manage and often remain hostile. They may refuse to eat for a period when first acquired, for example, and you should offer them a suitable variety of foods to encourage their appetites.

Males in particular may become aggressive during the breeding season, even when kept at a lower winter temperature. The eggs take about three months to hatch, and you will probably need to offer the young snakes small amphibians or fish at first until they can take larger prey, such as mammals and birds.

Elaphe guttata
Corn Snake
- **Distribution:** North America
- **Length:** 1.8m (6ft)
- **Diet:** Rodents
- **Ideal conditions:** Temperature 25-30°C (77-86°F)
- **Hibernation:** Provide a temperature of about 15-20°C (59-68°F) in winter
- **Sex differences:** Tail shape
- **Breeding:** Up to 20 eggs are likely

These snakes are justly popular and are ideal for beginners. They tame well and breed quite freely, and well-fed captive-bred stock is usually available. Corn Snakes do not need particularly spacious surroundings; a vivarium 100cm long, 50cm high and 50cm wide (39x20x20in) is fine for a pair. They feed quite readily on rodents.

They normally lay their eggs in the spring and they hatch after about two and a half months. Under normal circumstances, the young do not become mature until their second year.

Below: **Elaphe guttata**
Like other Elaphid snakes, this is a constrictor and varies in coloration.

Elaphe obsoleta
Rat Snakes
- **Distribution:** North America
- **Length:** Up to 2m (6.5ft)
- **Diet:** Rodents
- **Ideal conditions:** Vivarium temperature 25-30°C (77-86°F)
- **Hibernation:** Provide a winter temperature of around 15-20°C (59-68°F)
- **Sex differences:** Tail shape
- **Breeding:** Between 12 and 15 eggs are likely

The various subspecies of the Rat Snake differ widely in coloration, and the different colour forms are considered separate subspecies. Five variants are recognized: the Yellow Rat Snake (*Elaphe obsoleta quadriviltata*); the Everglades

Right: **Elaphe obsoleta**
This Texas Rat Snake is about to slough its skin, as shown by the cloudy appearance of the eyes.

Orange Rat Snake (*E.o.rossalleni*); the Grey Rat Snake (*E.o.spiloides*); the Black Rat Snake (*E.o.obsoleta*) and the Texas Rat Snake (*E.o.lindheimeri*). It is difficult to distinguish between the subspecies in young Rat Snakes, since at this stage they all appear similar.

Mating occurs during the spring, and the eggs are laid during the summer. The young snakes may be up to 40cm (16in) long when they hatch three months later. Rat Snakes are adept climbers; be sure to allow sufficient space in their quarters for this purpose.

Epicrates cenchria
Rainbow Boa
- **Distribution:** Central and South America
- **Length:** Up to 2m (6.5ft)
- **Diet:** Mammals and birds
- **Ideal conditions:** Minimum temperature around 24°C, rising to 30°C (75-86°F)
- **Hibernation:** No
- **Sex differences:** Males have bigger spurs than females
- **Breeding:** Less than 20 offspring are likely

The Rainbow Boa is one of the most colourful of the boids, particularly after shedding, when the iridescent new skin resembles a rainbow in

Above: **Epicrates cenchria**
A Rainbow Boa showing the typical iridescent markings along its sides.

appearance. The Brazilian subspecies is considered to be the most desirable, being mainly reddish in colour; other forms tend to be more brownish. These snakes are not difficult to maintain, but as you might expect they are relatively expensive.

Young Rainbow Boas are about 60cm (24in) long at birth, after a gestation period of about five months. Another member of the *Epicrates* genus, the Haitian Boa (*E.angulifer*), is also available from time to time and needs similar care.

Lampropeltis getulus

Common King Snake

- **Distribution:** North America
- **Length:** Up to 1.8m (6ft)
- **Diet:** Mice
- **Ideal conditions:** 24-30°C (75-86°F)
- **Hibernation:** Winter temperature around 10°C (50°F)
- **Sex differences:** Tail shape
- **Breeding:** Between 6 and 15 eggs are likely

King Snakes occur in various colour forms throughout their natural range. They are particularly active in the afternoon and evening, venturing forth in search of prey. An unusual characteristic of King Snakes is their readiness to devour other snakes, which has given rise to their common name. Indeed, they are reputed to be immune to the effects of rattlesnake venom. With this in mind, only keep individuals of the same size together, and ensure that these snakes are never overcrowded. When rearing young King Snakes, always supervise feeding to ensure that two individuals do not become locked on the same prey; this can precipitate cannibalism.

They will breed quite readily, mating in the spring and laying eggs in late summer. The eggs can take three months to hatch. It should be possible to rear the young successfully on pinkies (day-old mice). In the Californian King Snake (*L.g.californiae*) the markings of the offspring may be quite variable, with both banded and striped forms being produced in the same batch.

Below: **Lampropeltis getulus**
This is a fine striped specimen of the Californian King Snake.

Above: **Lampropeltis triangulum**
Another member of the genus that shows very variable coloration.

Lampropeltis triangulum
Milk Snake

- **Distribution:** North and Central America
- **Length:** Up to 120cm (4ft)
- **Diet:** Mice
- **Ideal conditions:** Vivarium temperature 25-30°C (77-86°F)
- **Hibernation:** Drop the temperature by 5-10°C (9-18°F) in winter
- **Sex differences:** Tail shape
- **Breeding:** Between 6 and 24 eggs are produced

These snakes are named after the early (and erroneous) belief that they fed upon milk. Again, there are various forms that show considerable diversity in coloration and which live in different environments. Some are found in arid areas; others live in damper environments. This variation in natural habitat is possibly the reason why the Milk Snake has gained a reputation for being one of the more sensitive members of the *Lampropeltis* genus to keep in captivity. Milk Snakes normally feed on mice, but they can also prove cannibalistic. They tend to be crepuscular in their habits (i.e. stirring at dawn and dusk) and are thus more active at low light levels. They have been bred repeatedly under vivarium conditions, producing up to 24 eggs in a clutch.

Natrix natrix

Grass Snake

- **Distribution:** Much of Europe, extending into Asia and northwestern Africa
- **Length:** Up to 2m (6.5ft)
- **Diet:** Amphibians and fish
- **Ideal conditions:** Temperature range 18-24°C (64-75°F)
- **Hibernation:** Yes
- **Sex differences:** Tail shape
- **Breeding:** Clutches may consist of up to 30 eggs

The wide distribution of this species demonstrates its adaptibility. Although described as a water snake, it spends much of its time on land. If not used to being handled, these snakes often expel a foul secretion from their cloacas. A further disconcerting action is its ability to appear dead. The snake coils its body loosely, remaining inert with its tongue hanging from its open mouth. Sometimes known as the 'Ringed Snake', several distinctive subspecies of the Grass Snake are recognized.

Below: **Natrix natrix**
A Grass Snake, showing the typical forked, very sensitive tongue found in snakes and some lizards.

Nerodia sipedon

Northern Water Snake

- **Distribution:** Eastern North America
- **Length:** Up to 120cm (4ft)
- **Diet:** Mainly fish and amphibians
- **Ideal conditions:** Temperature 25-30°C (77-86°F), falling during the winter
- **Hibernation:** Yes, for about three months (as with other species)
- **Sex differences:** Tail shape
- **Breeding:** About 15 young are produced

These snakes are easy to maintain in the vivarium, where they feed quite readily on whole fish and amphibians. As these are water snakes, provide a suitable water container in the vivarium. Always ensure, however, that they can enter the water bowl without flooding the surrounding area; do not fill the container to the brim. Mating takes place after hibernation, and the live young are produced during the summer.

Other species of *Nerodia*, such as the Red-bellied Water Snake (*N.erythrogaster*), are available from time to time; all need similar care.

Right: **Nerodia sipedon**
The Northern Water Snake spends some of its time in water, but must also have a dry area within its vivarium. They are not difficult to keep.

Pituophis melanoleucus
Pine, Gopher and Bull Snake
- **Distribution:** North America
- **Length:** Up to 2m (6.5ft)
- **Diet:** Rodents, especially mice
- **Ideal conditions:** 25-30°C (77-86°F) in the summer
- **Hibernation:** Yes
- **Sex differences:** Tail shape
- **Breeding:** As many as 12 eggs may be produced

The various common names for this snake have arisen because of the variations in its markings and coloration; they were first thought to be different species. These snakes are often rather nervous and aggressive when first acquired, but generally settle down without problems. Even if you keep them awake through the winter they may refuse to eat, so hibernation is recommended. They will breed after hibernation and the eggs take over two months to hatch. The young snakes moult once (as is usual with all species) and then start to feed. They are large enough at this stage to consume small rodents.

Below: **Pituophis melanoleucus**
Known under a variety of names. This is the Pacific Gopher (P.m. catenifer)

Ptyas mucosus

Asian Rat Snake

- **Distribution:** USSR to Southeast Asia
- **Length:** Up to 3.6m (12ft)
- **Diet:** Fish, amphibians and rodents
- **Ideal conditions:** Temperature 25-30°C (77-86°F)
- **Hibernation:** No
- **Sex differences:** Tail shape
- **Breeding:** Females lay up to 14 eggs in the wild

In the wild, these relatively large snakes pursue prey on the ground and in the trees. Unfortunately, they have not been bred successfully in captivity and specimens offered for sale are thus likely to be wild-caught. These should be carefully quarantined and treated for parasitic worms. The Indian Rat Snake (*P.kovcos*) is almost identical in its habits and requirements.

Below: **Ptyas mucosus**
The Asian Rat Snake – not yet as easy to breed as the American Rat Snakes.

Python molurus

Indian Python

- **Distribution:** Much of Asia
- **Length:** Up to 6.5m (21ft)
- **Diet:** Large rodents, rabbits, chickens as appropriate
- **Ideal conditions:** Temperature 25-30°C (77-86°F)
- **Hibernation:** No
- **Sex differences:** Males have more pronounced spurs than females
- **Breeding:** A clutch may consist of 50 eggs

There are two recognizable forms of this python, known as the light phase (*P.m.molurus*) and the dark phase (*P.m.bivittatus*). These are relatively easy snakes to maintain despite their large potential size, and will breed quite readily. Mating appears to be stimulated by a decrease in light and thus takes place in the winter. Afterwards, the female will lay the eggs within about three months, curling herself around them. Here she remains, until the eggs start to hatch about 70 days later. After their initial moult, the young pythons start to eat readily and can be mature 18 months later.

Right: **Python molurus**
Indian Pythons thrive in captivity and often breed in the vivarium.

Python regius
Royal Python

- **Distribution:** Africa
- **Length:** Up to 1.5m (5ft)
- **Diet:** Rodents, including gerbils
- **Ideal conditions:** Temperature 25-30°C (77-86°F)
- **Hibernation:** No
- **Sex differences:** Males have more pronounced spurs than females
- **Breeding:** A clutch may consist of eight eggs

These colourful pythons are also known as Ball Pythons, since they curl up tightly into a ball when they are threatened, with the head inside. Although attractive, they can be difficult snakes to maintain because they enter periods of prolonged fasting. Mice are generally the preferred prey. Although it is possible to force-feed them, this needs expert guidance.

Above: **Python regius**
Royal Pythons are not the easiest pythons to maintain successfully.

Thamnophis sauritus

Eastern Ribbon Snake

- **Distribution:** North America
- **Length:** Up to 80cm (31in)
- **Diet:** Mainly fish
- **Ideal conditions:** Temperature 22-26°C (72-79°F)
- **Hibernation:** Yes
- **Sex differences:** Pregnant females appear swollen
- **Breeding:** Brood size 20-30

Closely related to the Garter Snakes, the Ribbon Snakes are also semi-terrestrial in their habits, but have even thinner bodies and tend to prove more nervous. Ribbon Snakes may often refuse earthworms, preferring fish and amphibians as the basis of their diet. In order to prevent the risk of a thiamin (Vitamin B) deficiency, cook whole fish offered as food lightly to inactivate the thiaminase enzyme that destroys this vitamin. Nervous signs – typically shaking and lack of co-ordination – are the result of a thiamin deficiency. Alternatively, supplement the diet with a vitamin and mineral preparation (usually a powder) to help prevent these effects.

Above: **Thamnophis sauritus**
Ribbon Snakes produce live young. In the wild, they mate in early spring.

Below: **Thamnophis sirtalis**
The widely distributed subspecies of

Thamnophis sirtalis
Common Garter Snake
- **Distribution:** North America
- **Length:** Up to 120cm (4ft)
- **Diet:** Fish, earthworms and small amphibians
- **Ideal conditions:** Dry surroundings, temperature 22-26°C (72-79°F) in summer
- **Hibernation:** Yes
- **Sex differences:** Pregnant females appear swollen
- **Breeding:** About 8 to 30 young can be expected

the Common Garter Snake vary in their habitat and feeding preferences.

There is considerable diversity in the markings of Garter Snakes, so-called because of their slender shape. They are easy to cater for and the young are not difficult to rear. The western subspecies – the most colourful forms – differ from other races in their habits, being more aquatic and inclined to feed on fish rather than on earthworms.

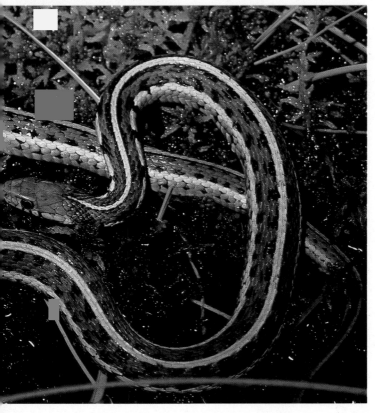

Frogs and Toads

Class AMPHIBIA: The Amphibians
There are two major Orders within this Class, all members of which are closely dependent on water, especially for breeding purposes. The Order Anura embraces the frogs and toads; as a general rule, those species belonging to the genus *Bufo* are described as toads, whereas members of the genus *Rana* are referred to as frogs. There is some confusion, however, in the case of other genera. In the Order Caudata (literally meaning tailed amphibians) there is no clear distinction between the two categories of newts and salamanders; both common names are often interchanged.

Bombina bombina
Fire-bellied Toad
- **Distribution:** Eastern Europe, extending into Western Asia
- **Length:** 5cm (2in)
- **Diet:** Small invertebrates and earthworms
- **Ideal conditions:** Very aquatic. Temperature about 21°C(70°F)
- **Hibernation:** Yes
- **Sex differences:** Males have a more slender profile than females
- **Breeding:** 100 or so eggs in a single spawning

These toads are more aquatic than close relatives such as the Oriental Fire-bellied Toad (*B.orientalis*). A tank containing relatively shallow

Above: **Bombina orientalis**
Both Oriental and Common Fire-bellied Toads will breed readily in the vivarium. Eggs hatch in two weeks.

water and some floating plants provides the ideal environment; adult frogs can be housed out of doors during the summer months. The red coloration of the belly can become pale without colour feeding; use the fish foods specifically produced for this purpose.

Young Fire-bellied Toads are likely to breed during their second year. Increasing the light level appears to stimulate breeding activity in these amphibians.

Order: ANURA – Frogs and Toads
This is a very large Order, consisting of approximately 2,000 species split into 17 Families. Most anurans live in the tropics. With their relatively dry warty skins, the toads tend to be better adapted for life on land than the frogs. (These swellings are not warts, however, and – contrary to superstition – they cannot be transmitted to anyone handling these anurans.) Toads tend to walk more than frogs, which favour a hopping mode of locomotion. The more aquatic species have webbing between the toes of the hind feet; the tree-living species have disc-shaped climbing pads.

Bufo marinus
Giant Toad
- **Distribution:** Central and South America
- **Length:** 20cm (8in)
- **Diet:** Invertebrates and even pinkies
- **Ideal conditions:** Adequate substrate for burrowing
- **Hibernation:** No
- **Sex differences:** Females can be twice as large as males
- **Breeding:** Several thousand eggs may be laid during the year

Handle these large toads with care, since they have parotid glands on the head which produce a toxic secretion. It is safer to wear gloves, especially if you have cuts on your hands. They are not difficult to cater for in captivity. They are mainly terrestrial and will burrow into the substrate of their vivarium. Always provide a small bowl of water in their enclosure, however; these toads will survive in brackish water, but are by nature a freshwater species.

The Giant Toad has been introduced to areas where sugar cane is grown in a bid to control the grey cane beetles. Unfortunately, it has failed to control these pests and in some localities is a pest itself.

Below: **Bufo marinus**
Giant Toads are easy to keep, but some may prove reluctant to feed.

Dendrobates species

Poison Arrow Frogs

- **Distribution:** Central and South America
- **Length:** 2.5-4cm (1-1.6in)
- **Diet:** Small invertebrates
- **Ideal conditions:** Heated, planted vivarium
- **Hibernation:** No
- **Sex differences:** Males have vocal slits
- **Breeding:** A single spawning may consist of 13 eggs

The Poison Arrow Frogs rank among the most expensive of frogs to buy, but they make fascinating and beautiful vivarium occupants. They are so named because of their toxic skin secretions, which native Indians use (in concentrated form) to tip their arrows. Needless to say, avoid handling these frogs directly; wear gloves if you do need to handle them. The Poison Arrow Frogs will thrive in a well-planted vivarium and they need only a shallow dish of water to supply essential moisture.

Males establish distinct territories – in which they call and display to prospective mates – and are likely to prove aggressive towards other males. There is no amplexus and the eggs are fertilized where they are laid, on the ground. The adult male collects the eggs and carries them on his back until he deposits the tadpoles in a suitable puddle to complete their development. Other related species are grouped in the genera *Phyllobates* and *Sminthillus*.

Below: **Dendrobates histrionicus**
The markings of this colourful Poison Arrow Frog are variable. This species is often available from dealers.

Hyla arborea
European Tree Frog

- **Distribution:** Europe and Asia
- **Length:** Up to 5cm (2in)
- **Diet:** Small invertebrates
- **Ideal conditions:** Tall, planted vivarium
- **Hibernation:** Yes
- **Sex differences:** Males are thinner than females at breeding time
- **Breeding:** As many as 1,000 eggs can result from a single spawning

Above: **Hyla arborea**
Flies are a favourite food for the elegant European Tree Frog.

There are a large number of tree frogs. All have modified feet that enable them to climb vertical surfaces. They spend most of their time in trees and may even breed in pools in tree forks. This particular species is hardy and easy to keep. It does well at liberty in a greenhouse during the summer. It is much more likely to breed under these conditions, particularly if it has access to a reasonable area of water with plants growing in and around it to simulate a pond.

Hyla cinerea
Green Tree Frog

- **Distribution:** Southeastern United States
- **Length:** Up to 6.25cm (2.5in)
- **Diet:** Small invertebrates
- **Ideal conditions:** A tall vivarium
- **Hibernation:** No
- **Sex differences:** Males are thinner than females during the breeding season
- **Breeding:** A relatively large number of eggs is produced; about 500

This is one of the New World counterparts of the European Tree Frog and is similar in its habits and requirements, although this

Above: **Hyla cinerea**
This species from the USA is less hardy than its European counterpart.

particular species tends to be more active. The Green Tree Frog can sometimes be confused with the Squirrel Tree Frog (*H.squirella*). Both occur in the same area and are similar in coloration and appearance. The main distinguishing feature of the latter species is that the stripe runs from the eye only as far as the forelegs.

A number of other American *Hyla* species, such as the Spring Peeper (*H.crucifer*) and the Common Tree Frog (*H.versicolor*), are also kept occasionally by enthusiasts.

Megophrys nasuta
Asiatic Horned Toad
- **Distribution:** Southeast Asia
- **Length:** Up to 10cm (4in)
- **Diet:** Invertebrates
- **Ideal conditions:** A terrestrial vivarium heated to about 25°C (77°F)
- **Hibernation:** No
- **Sex differences:** Females may be larger than males
- **Breeding:** No records exist

This species is one of the horned toads that occur in various parts of the world. The horns consist of skin folds above the eyes and on the nose. These creatures are essentially forest dwellers, where they remain buried for long periods. Horned toads are invariably highly aggressive and so be sure to keep individuals of different sizes well apart to prevent cannibalism.

Below: **Megophrys nasuta**
The Asiatic Horned Toad. The tadpoles of this species are said to be essentially vegetarian, unlike those of their South American relatives.

Pelobates fuscus
Spadefoot Toad
- **Distribution:** Europe
- **Length:** 6.25cm (2.5in)
- **Diet:** Insects
- **Ideal conditions:** A deep sandy substrate in the vivarium
- **Hibernation:** Yes
- **Sex differences:** Females are more rotund than males
- **Breeding:** Several hundred eggs may be laid

In common with the Horned Toad, this is a member of the Spadefoot Toad Family. Using the projections on the side of the hind feet, this species escapes potential predators by digging very rapidly to conceal itself. This is the most common of the three European species; very similar toads of the genus *Scaphiopus* occur in the

Above: **Pelobates cultripes**
The Spanish Spadefoot Toad. As with Pelobates fuscus, *rainfall appears to trigger breeding activity.*

United States. Spadefoot Toads can be difficult to maintain successfully under vivarium conditions and will remain hidden from view for long periods.

Rana catesbeiana
Bullfrog

- **Distribution:** North America
- **Length:** 20cm (8in)
- **Diet:** Insects, pinkies and (for larger individuals) adult mice
- **Ideal conditions:** Large enclosure in view of their size, temperature in excess of 15°C (59°F)
- **Hibernation:** Yes
- **Sex differences:** The eardrum is significantly larger in males than in females
- **Breeding:** A large amount of spawn is produced

These big frogs tend to live solitary lives, but their characteristic calls echo around the ponds where they live. When you first obtain them they tend to be shy, but if you provide adequate cover they will settle in well. Bullfrogs have large appetites and some individuals can be persuaded to take pinkies. Again, they do show cannibalistic tendencies if you keep different sizes of individuals together in a group. Their life cycle is relatively slow, since the tadpoles may remain in the larval stage for as long as two years before they finally metamorphose into adults.

Below: **Rana catesbeiana**
These bullfrogs are a highly aquatic species, but hibernate on land.

Rana temporaria

Common Frog

- **Distribution:** Eurasia
- **Length:** Up to 10cm (4in)
- **Diet:** Insects
- **Ideal conditions:** Temperature about 17°C (63°F) in summer
- **Hibernation:** Yes
- **Sex differences:** Males develop nuptial pads on the forelegs during the breeding season
- **Breeding:** Spawn is laid in clumps

Although typically ranid in appearance, the Common Frog is quite variable in its coloration. In captivity they tend to be rather nervous, and may injure their snouts by jumping at the glass if kept closely confined without adequate cover. In many areas, it is best to keep Common Frogs in an outdoor enclosure, where collective spawning can take place during the spring. As the number of traditional breeding sites declines, it is vital to encourage these creatures to breed in other localities, such as garden ponds. Common Frogs rarely stray far from water throughout the year, in contrast to the Common Toad (*Bufo bufo*), which only visits water for breeding purposes.

Below: **Rana temporaria**
Keep Common Frogs outdoors.

Xenopus laevis
African Clawed Toad

- **Distribution:** Southern Africa
- **Length:** Up to 12.5cm (5in)
- **Diet:** Worms and insects
- **Ideal conditions:** Shallow, warm aquatic environment at about 25°C(77°F)
- **Hibernation:** No
- **Sex differences:** Males are smaller than females and lack the anal papillae (swellings close to the cloaca)
- **Breeding:** In excess of 500 eggs can result from a single spawning

These toads have been used for laboratory purposes since the 1930s, when it was realised that they could perform a vital role in pregnancy testing. Injecting female

Above: **Xenopus laevis**
The African Clawed Toad – a widely known truly aquatic species.

Xenopus with the urine of pregnant women causes them to produce eggs within 18 hours. This method, although now superseded, proved reliable and guaranteed the popularity of *Xenopus*.

These are truly aquatic toads that will breed easily, but, again, can become cannibalistic. Young *Xenopus* tadpoles grow quite large, and feed on particles in suspension; use the foods developed for fish fry to rear them. It has proved possible to use synthetic hormones to encourage breeding in this species, and this technique has now been refined for use with other anurans.

107

Newts and Salamanders

Order: CAUDATA – Newts and Salamanders
Members of this Order are fairly uniform in appearance; all have cylindrical bodies, short legs and a relatively long tail. They vary in size, however. The largest are the giant salamanders of the species *Andrias* from China and Japan; they can grow to length of about 1.45m(4.4ft). A related form known as the Hellbender *(Cryptobranchus alleganiensis)* occurs in the USA and reaches 45cm(18in) in length. None of the caudates available as pets reaches these sizes, however, and so they are quite suitable for keeping in vivariums of modest dimensions in the average home.

Ambystoma mexicanum
Axolotl

- **Distribution:** Mexico
- **Length:** Up to 30cm (12in)
- **Diet:** Earthworms, small pieces of meat
- **Ideal conditions:** Must be kept under aquatic conditions
- **Hibernation:** No
- **Sex differences:** Males have swollen cloacas
- **Breeding:** Up to 500 eggs

The Axolotl is a bizarre creature. It is an extreme example of the phenomenon known as neoteny, which means that it becomes sexually mature and is able to reproduce in its larval form. Indeed, it will spend all of its life in this state if kept under aquatic conditions. Should it undergo metamorphosis (triggered by the drying up of the pool), the Axolotl is transformed into a creature known as the Mexican Salamander.

Two colour variants of the Axolotl are recognized: an albino and a black form. They are easy to keep and need no decor in their tank of warm water. Axolotls will readily take earthworms and even small pieces of meat, although you must be sure to keep the aquarium clean of uneaten foodstuffs.

They become sexually mature at the age of a year and a half, and the characteristic sperm packets, or spermatophores, produced by the male are caught by the female. As the eggs hatch, you may need to separate the young Axolotls to prevent overcrowding. Otherwise, injuries from fighting are likely, and although limbs can be regenerated, there is always the risk of a fatal infection occurring. Both colour forms can be anticipated in the brood, depending on the parents.

Above and below:
Ambystoma mexicanum
The albino and black forms of the fascinating Axolotl, with feathery gills.

Ambystoma tigrinum
Tiger Salamander

- **Distribution:** North America
- **Length:** 17cm(7in) average; some can reach 30cm(12in) in certain localities
- **Diet:** Large invertebrates, worms
- **Ideal conditions:** Vivarium temperature 15-25°C (59-77°F)
- **Hibernation:** If required
- **Sex differences:** Cloacal region, and males are slimmer than females overall
- **Breeding:** Small numbers of eggs are laid in succession

This is a typical member of the group known as Mole Salamanders. They tend to be rather shy in their habits, but will settle well under vivarium conditions where they have adequate cover and a small pool. They will feed on relatively large invertebrates, including worms. If eggs are produced, these will hatch in about six weeks. Rear the young on whiteworm and similar live foods; they should grow rapidly.

Below: **Ambystoma tigrinum**
A striking, if rather shy species.

Cynops pyrrhogaster
Japanese Fire-bellied Newt
- ● **Distribution:** Japan
- ● **Length:** Up to 10cm (4in)
- ● **Diet:** Insects
- ● **Ideal conditions:** Relatively cool (about 20°C/68°F), unpolluted water
- ● **Hibernation:** Yes, it may prove essential for breeding
- ● **Sex differences:** Males gain a purplish sheen on their tails and are slimmer than females
- ● **Breeding:** Small numbers of eggs

This is one of the various oriental newts that are available on an

Above: **Cynops pyrrhogaster**
The Japanese Fire-bellied Newt. These newts are easy to cater for, and will even learn to take small pieces of meat dropped into the water. They must be kept in clean water, however, with no excess meat left in the tank.

almost regular basis. They are highly attractive, with bright orange-red underparts. They are undemanding to maintain, being hardy and easy to feed. They are not easy to breed, however. A densely planted tank may offer the best chance of breeding success, and you may need to experiment with the vegetation for the best results.

Salamandra salamandra
Fire Salamander

- **Distribution:** Southern Europe, extending into Asia
- **Length:** Up to 19cm (7.5in), occasionally much bigger
- **Diet:** Insects
- **Ideal conditions:** Cool surroundings, not exceeding 20°C (68°F)
- **Hibernation:** Yes
- **Sex differences:** Males are thinner than females
- **Breeding:** Up to 40 young may be produced

The boldly coloured Fire Salamander is poisonous, since it exudes a toxic secretion known as salamandrin from pores behind the eyes. Do not handle it unnecessarily, and use gloves if you need to. It is more terrestrial than other salamanders; it mates on land and the eggs are retained in the female's body until they are ready to hatch. This takes place over the winter period, and the young finally appear during the spring of the following year. The young salamanders leave the water about two months later and are able to live an independent existence on land.

Below: **Salamandra salamandra**
A number of legends have grown up about Fire Salamanders. In the 17th century it was widely believed that they possessed a fatal bite and were able to extinguish fires!

Triturus cristatus
Crested Newt
- **Distribution:** Europe
- **Length:** 15cm (6in)
- **Diet:** Insects and other invertebrates
- **Ideal conditions:** Must be able to leave the water
- **Hibernation:** Yes
- **Sex differences:** Males have a tall crest during the breeding season
- **Breeding:** The numerous eggs are deposited on the under-surfaces of aquatic plant leaves

Crested Newts are easy to cater for, feeding readily on suitable invertebrates or inert matter offered to them. The male is particularly resplendent during the breeding season in spring. Later, Crested Newts will seek to leave the water and must be allowed to do so. Although they can be kept in water throughout the year, successive breeding results are poor. Newts are not above eating their own tadpoles, so be sure to establish separate rearing quarters.

In some areas, such as in the UK, the natural population of Crested Newts has declined so much that their collection from the wild is not permitted, except under licence.

Right: **Triturus cristatus**
A pair of Giant Crested Newts, the male seen here above the female. They can produce a poisonous skin secretion from glands along the back to deter potential predators.

Triturus vulgaris
Smooth Newt
- **Distribution:** Europe
- **Length:** Up to 9cm (3.5in)
- **Diet:** Insects
- **Ideal conditions:** Provide both land and water in the vivarium
- **Hibernation:** Yes
- **Sex differences:** Males develop a crest in the breeding season
- **Breeding:** As many as 200 eggs may be produced

As with other European species, you should keep Smooth Newts in cool water at about 16°C (61°F). It is very easy to confuse this species with the Palmate Newt (*Triturus helveticus*), although males – with the numerous spots on their underparts – are relatively easy to distinguish; females can prove more difficult. Females of both species have orange bellies, but in Smooth Newts this is a deeper colour than in Palmate females. Both species require similar care to that recommended for Crested Newts.

Left: **Triturus vulgaris**
The Smooth Newt can be kept in an outdoor enclosure, with adequate cover and water available. The description of 'newt' is derived from the Anglo-Saxon word for these amphibians, 'evete', which became altered to 'ewt', and finally 'newt'.

Index to species

Page numbers in **bold** indicate major references, including accompanying photographs. Page numbers in *italics* indicate captions to other illustrations. Less important text entries are shown in normal type.

115

Further reading

Alderton, D. *Tortoises and Terrapins* Saiga Publishing, 1980
Bellairs, A. *The Life of Reptiles* Weidenfeld and Nicolson, 1969
Breen, J.F. *Encyclopedia of Reptiles and Amphibians* TFH Publications, 1974
Cochran, D.M. *Living Amphibians of the World* Doubleday/Hamish Hamilton, 1961
Cooper, J.E. & Jackson, O.F. *Diseases of the Reptilia* Academic Press, 1981
Fitch, H.S. *Reproductive Cycles in Lizards and Snakes* University of Kansas, Museum of
    Natural History, 1970
Gans, C. *Reptiles of the World* Ridge Press/Bantam Books, 1975
Griehl, K. *Snakes – Giant Snakes and Non-venomous Snakes in the Terrarium* Barron's
    Educational Series Inc., 1984
Mattison, C. *The Care of Reptiles and Amphibians in Captivity* Blandford Press, 1982
Murphy, J.B. & Collins, J.T. (Eds.) *Reproductive Biology and Diseases of Captive
    Reptiles* Society for the Study of Amphibians and Reptiles, 1980
Pritchard, P.C.H. *Encyclopedia of Turtles* TFH Publications, 1979
Riches, R.J. *Breeding Snakes in Captivity* Arco, 1976
Schmidt, K.P. & Inger, R.F. *Living Reptiles of the World* Doubleday/Hamish Hamilton,
    1957
Townson, S., et al (Eds.) *The Care and Breeding of Captive Reptiles* British
    Herpetological Society, 1980
Wilke, H. *Turtles – A Complete Pet Owner's Manual* Barron's Educational Series Inc.,
    1983

In addition, many articles on the management and breeding of herptiles appear in *The International Zoo Yearbook* published annually.

Useful addresses

Herpetological societies exist in many countries around the world. This selection lists the principal societies in the UK and the USA:

UK
Association for the Study of Reptiles and Amphibians (ASRA),
c/o The Cotswold Wildlife Park, BURFORD, Oxfordshire OX8 4JW.

British Herpetological Society (BHS),
c/o The Zoological Society of London, Regent's Park, LONDON NW1 4RY.

International Herpetological Society (IHS),
65 Broadstone Avenue, WALSALL, West Midlands WS3 1JA.

USA
Society for the Study of Amphibians and Reptiles (SSAR),
c/o Department of Zoology, Miami University, OXFORD, Ohio 45056.

Picture credits

Artists
Copyright of the artwork illustrations on the pages following the artists' names is the property of Salamander Books Ltd.

Clifford and Wendy Meadway: 14-5, 21, 22-3, 24, 26, 28, 30, 32, 34-5, 38, 44, 49, 50, 53

Colin Newman (Linden Artists): 45

Brian Watson (Linden Artists): 33

Photographs
The publishers wish to thank the following photographers and agencies who have supplied photographs for this book. The photographs have been credited by page number and position on the page: (B) Bottom, (T) Top, (C) Centre, (BL) Bottom left etc.

David Alderton: 16-7(T), 68

Heather Angel/Biofotos: 94, 100, 104(B)

Ardea: 10-11 (Alan Weaving), 29(John Mason), 74-5(B, Pat Morris), 110-11(T, Pat Morris), 113(T, John Clegg)

Michael Chinery 12(T)

John Coborn © Routedale Ltd: 64(B), 91(T)

Bruce Coleman Ltd: 15, 62, 63, 67(T, Jack Dermid), 69(B, Jack Dermid), 82-3(B), 95(B, Jack Dermid), 106-7(T, Jane Burton), 109(C), 112-3(B, Jane Burton)

Eric Crichton © Salamander Books: 25, 33

David Hosking: 66

Frank Lane Picture Agency Ltd: 96

Jan-Eric Larsson: 39

Keith Lawrence: 55, 56(T,B), 57, 58, 59

Chris Mattison: Endpapers, Title page, Copyright page, 18(B), 19, 26, 27, 47, 51, 64(T), 72(B), 78, 79(C,B) 83(T), 84, 85(B), 86(T), 89, 90, 91(B), 92-3(B), 93(T), 95(C), 96-7(T), 98-9(T,B), 101, 103(T), 104(T), 105, 106(B), 108(T), 111(B)

Arend van den Nieuwenhuizen: Half-title page, 18(T), 22-3, 36, 41, 65, 69(C), 70, 71(B), 72-3, 76, 80, 85(T), 86-7(B), 97(B), 103(C)

Don Reid: 40, 48, 67(B), 71(T)

Peter W. Scott: 17, 34, 45, 52, 53, 54, 108-9(B)

W.A. Tomey: 12(B), 13, 20, 30, 31, 37, 46, 60-1, 77, 81, 102

The Zoological Society of London: 75(T), 88

Acknowledgements
The publishers wish to thank Rita Hemsley, Keith Lawrence and Phil Reid for their help in preparing this book.

Companion volumes of interest:

A Fishkeeper's Guide to THE TROPICAL AQUARIUM
A Fishkeeper's Guide to COMMUNITY FISHES
A Fishkeeper's Guide to COLDWATER FISHES
A Fishkeeper's Guide to MARINE FISHES
A Fishkeeper's Guide to MAINTAINING A HEALTHY AQUARIUM
A Fishkeeper's Guide to GARDEN PONDS
A Fishkeeper's Guide to CENTRAL AMERICAN CICHLIDS

Chrysemys scripta elegans (*Red-eared Slider*)

PRINTED IN BELGIUM BY

INTERNATIONAL BOOK PRODUCTION